DRIVEN *by* COMPASSION

www.amplifypublishing.com

Driven by Compassion: 8 Values for Successful Servant Leaders

For more information, please contact:
Amplify, an imprint of Amplify Publishing Group
620 Herndon Parkway, Suite 320
Herndon, VA 20170
info@amplifypublishing.com

Library of Congress Control Number: 2021912774

CPSIA Code: PRV0322A

ISBN-13: 978-1-64543-667-6

Printed in the United States

This book is dedicated to my wife and life partner, Rhonda, and my daughters, Audra and Alyssa, who sacrificed and supported our many family relocations to support my leadership career. My career and this book would not have happened without their love and patience, for which I am eternally grateful.

DRIVEN
by
COMPASSION

8 VALUES FOR
Successful Servant Leaders

DAVID ZECHMAN

amplify

CONTENTS

FOREWORD

DRIVEN BY COMPASSION: 8 VALUES FOR SUCCESSFUL SERVANT LEADERS is the right book at the right time.

When I read David's opening line about a "leadership style that will help you 'remember, refresh, and renew' why you decided to accept the awesome responsibility of leading an organization's most valuable resource for success," it resonated on a heart level. This is a message that people need to hear right now.

I recently wrote a book on a similar subject. Titled *The Calling: Why Healthcare Is So Special*, it's about helping healthcare people connect to their own sense of purpose and passion . . . the "why" that keeps them going in every day and doing their best to be helpful and useful.

Keeping tuned into that sense of calling—whether you're a leader or an employee—isn't always easy. Healthcare has always been a tough industry. COVID-19 has made it even tougher. While healthcare people are truly exceptional human beings, it's hard to stay focused on passion and purpose in times of great stress and uncertainty.

Yet right now, when everyone is struggling, it's more crucial than ever to keep that passion and purpose on the front burner. Leaders need to a) keep our own emotional bank account filled and b) make more deposits into the emotional bank accounts of our employees (and fewer withdrawals). It's not just a nice thing to do. It's a matter of survival.

Today, we know that there's a powerful link between employee engagement and the patient experience, and that both are connected to clinical quality. Healthcare organizations regularly track these metrics. Yet if we could rewind the world a few decades, we would find a different reality. We likely wouldn't hear as much discussion around passion, purpose, and making a difference. Books like this one—which center on concepts like patience, trust, vulnerability, and forgiveness—might not find as much of an audience.

It's not that our industry didn't care. Healthcare has always been filled with deeply caring, mission-driven people. It's that leaders were grappling with complex financial issues and a rapidly changing industry landscape. They were pulled in so many directions that what were (at the time) considered "soft" issues just weren't top of mind. It hadn't yet clicked that tapping into people's sense of calling, connecting to their most deeply held values, and keeping their emotional bank accounts full are actually what drive results and organizational performance.

The point I'm getting to is this: I'm truly grateful this shift in our understanding and leadership priorities has taken place. Not only does it feel better to lead the way David describes in this book, it fuels people in a way nothing else can. Without compassionate values as our foundation, we may not have made it through the past couple of years.

What's more, when we lead with love and compassion, we impact not only our employees but ourselves. When leaders work hard to treat others with patience, build trust, and embody servant leadership—and put into practice the eight values David writes about—we get better on the inside. It's only when we get our inside right that we can be more successful on the outside. It all works together.

I hope you will enjoy David's book as much as I did. It's filled with practical, tactical, easy-to-understand guidance. That, along with its conversational tone and manageable length, make it the perfect read for overwhelmed healthcare professionals. It's a great book to share with your entire team. Not only is it filled with helpful leadership nuggets, it's a wonderful resource for helping reconnect everyone to their passion and sense of purpose.

Most of all, it serves as the gentle reminder we all need right now: love and compassion are what really matter, not just in the workplace but in all areas of life. This book shows us how to put them at the center of our leadership.

Quint Studer
Author of *The Calling: Why Healthcare Is So Special*

FOREWORD

AS I SAT DOWN TO write this foreword, I honestly didn't know where to start. And I'm a writer by trade. But how exactly do you put into words how much someone has impacted your life? Especially when that someone is your dad. Yes, this is a foreword for my dad's book on servant leadership, so full disclosure, this will not exactly be "unbiased," but it will give you a sense of who he is as a leader through his daughter's eyes. But I also think I will be channeling a lot of others' opinions of his leadership skills as well, otherwise we wouldn't be here. So I am going to try and do this man justice and make him proud with the best foreword I can think of for the best leader I know. So here goes—Dad, I am so proud to be your daughter, and I know this book and your story will help so many others on their path to becoming a true leader.

Let's be honest, I've looked up to my dad since day one. Not just because he is my dad, but because I have gotten to see him become a true servant leader throughout his career. Our family proudly has been a part of that path and moved around quite a bit in my childhood to make that happen. And it's worthy to note, my mom sacrificed a lot to support his dreams, and I'd be remiss if I did not mention the powerful woman behind this man. She stayed at home with us, helped us get acclimated to new schools, carted us around for sports, etc., as my dad followed his dreams to become a world class leader in healthcare. Thank you, Mom. "Superhero" doesn't begin to cover it.

I love the term "servant leadership" and all that comes with it, and we'll get into specifically why my dad exhibits these qualities. Let's backtrack to 2008, when I was an intern in the hospital where he was CEO. It was a small town, and everyone knew each other. Everyone knew my dad, but that's not really the important part here. What's important is this: I have a specific memory of walking down the hall with my dad at the hospital for my internship, and even though it was a small hospital, it was a decent-sized staff. I kid you not, every single hospital worker who walked by us, my dad said hello to them by name. He never missed a single person. It may seem small, but I assure you, as someone who has worked for a lot of CEOs, this is a big deal and can mean the world to someone walking by. I know it did to me. He knew everyone's names, from the doctors to the gift shop volunteers.

I would also listen to him speak at staff meetings, and yes, I would fangirl pretty hard, as I was so proud of him. But one thing I noticed that he did was that he truly engaged with everyone in the room and listened to what they had to say, not just talked at them. He also always led with inspiration in everything he did. He would send out weekly emails to his entire staff with inspirational thoughts to start and end a week. I know the CEOs who have done that in my experience, and it makes a difference.

Servant leadership is more than numbers. And my dad knew

that; he lived by that. Sure, he had numbers to hit; we all do. You can't ignore the numbers, but you can't let the numbers dictate how you lead. You need to take a step back and look at the bigger picture—the people behind the numbers. Like I said, I've worked for a lot of different types of leaders in my time as well. Some good, some not so good. Very few have known my name, if we are being honest. And I don't think I ever thought about the fact that you can lead with love and compassion. More importantly, that you should. Your employees are people, not numbers. And I saw that with my dad. I don't think this is a widely-known concept— leading with love. It sounds foreign and not something you would tie your leadership style to, but I'm here to tell you, you can. It's about seeing your team, really seeing them for who they are and allowing them to grow. Everyone wants to be seen and heard, and a true leader puts the needs of their team before their own. Be a servant to your team.

My dad is a true servant leader. He believes if you set your people up for success, you will be set up for success. In my current role, I am responsible for leading a team as well, and I use him as an example every day of how to lead. And believe me, I still have a lot to learn.

My dad is not only a true servant to his employees, but he is a servant of God. And I believe without a shadow of a doubt that this conviction has only helped him grow as a selfless leader. Don't get me wrong, we all have our moments, leaders or not, that prompt us to be selfish, make mistakes, et cetera. No one except God is perfect. But having that conviction grounds you and helps you to see what is important, what matters. My dad believes that you stay dedicated to your values, no matter what happens, which is really hard to do in today's world. But he has done it as a leader, and I hope he'll help other leaders to see through this lens of love and compassion. "Do as I *do*." Not "do what I say, not as I do." Let that sink in.

One of the key values that you will learn in this book that has really stuck out to me is: grudgeless—be willing to forgive. I thought about this for a long time. And something occurred to me: I don't think it's just being willing to forgive those who you lead. I think it's being willing to forgive yourself. Forgive yourself as a leader. You will make mistakes; you will fail. Leaders are under a lot of pressure to succeed, but what comes with that is a bunch of failures before you truly succeed. And that's okay, be willing to forgive. Forgive yourself, forgive others, and work as a team to achieve a goal.

I'm going to end with a story about something that made me roll my eyes all the time as a kid. Just bear with me for a sec, trust me. My mom and dad had a magnet they put on the fridge that said, "Do the right thing." I kid you not, we heard it all the time and that magnet was with us until I graduated high school. Honestly, they probably still have it, and I'm a grown woman. Not that I didn't want to do the right thing when I was younger, but I didn't need to hear it all the time! But I get it now. And I'm telling you this because my dad has stood by that conviction both as a parent and his entire career as a leader. So simple in theory, but not so much in practice.

If you think about it, it shouldn't be that hard to do: lead with love and compassion. But it truly is a challenge in this crazy, fast-paced world we live in. Why else would we be here writing this book? But those kinds of leaders, once cultivated, will change the world and leave it a better place than they found it. Trust us. And read on.

And what kind of leader will stand the test of time? My dad. I'm here to tell you, you will come away from this book a changed leader, for the better. Now go out and change the world, just like my dad.

Audra Zechman Felten

INTRODUCTION

WELCOME TO A LEADERSHIP STYLE that will help you "remember, refresh, and renew" why you decided to accept the awesome responsibility to lead an organization's most valuable resource for success—its people. The title of this exciting book emphasizes eight values that will motivate those who desire to be successful servant leaders. The amazing, loving, and compassionate values that embody this philosophy are the following:

- Patience
- Trustful
- Grudgeless
- Honesty and Integrity
- Communication
- Servant Leadership
- Walk the Talk
- Commitment

Incorporating these eight values into your leadership life will assuredly make a positive difference in the lives you affect in the workplace and improve organizational performance.

Where I am coming from

I spent much of my professional career in leadership positions in healthcare organizations, including serving as CEO at two hospitals, but I actually trace my approach to a leadership style that prioritizes compassion to when I was a high school track and football coach. I realized then that if I was going to be able to get the maximum performance out of those young men that would most benefit them and their development, then I could not use the old coaching style of yelling, screaming, and negative reinforcement. I instead was going to have to focus on positive reinforcement. I worked to make sure every kid knew that they belonged on the team—that they were a crucial member of the team—whether they were a superstar or not. It became clear to me that it was essential to show these kids that I genuinely cared about each of them, no matter their abilities, and that was the best way to help them dedicate themselves to the task at hand. The experience was a formative part of my life that I will always treasure.

Over the years, I have had some influential mentors who have helped steer me down a path of compassionate, servant leadership. One was Philip Weintraub, a brilliant man who served as the deputy director of the Federal Reserve Bank in the Reagan Administration. I got to know Philip when I was leading a hospital in Palm Beach County, Florida, and his genuine compassion for people and his dedication to helping them through leadership was an inspiration to me.

Another crucial mentor to me was Douglas Shaw, the president of Jewish Hospital in Louisville, Kentucky. I reported to Doug when I was managing the Heart and Lung Institute at that hospital, and Doug taught me to always act and look professionally, no matter the circumstances, and to talk to people whenever possible—rather than lean on email or other shortcuts. Live communication was critical to Doug, and I'll never forget the time he scolded me for starting to write an email to a colleague on a critical issue, saying, "Put the computer away and walk over there and talk to them. A face-to-face conversation will mean more."

The last of the mentors that most influenced me was Philip Incarnati, president and CEO of McLaren Health Care in Michigan. One thing I admired about Phil—something I took to heart in my own approach to leadership—was that Phil always had time for you, even though he was the CEO of a $6 billion company. I served as one of McLaren's fourteen hospital CEOs, and I could call Phil for feedback, and he would always help, though I did not even directly report to him. He would always make time, despite having precious little of it, and he would always give you his full attention.

One leader I do not know personally who has had an impact on me is former football coach Lou Holtz. I am a big sports fan, and I always admired Holtz's teams. Holtz had a straightforward philosophy he espoused: "Do the right thing. Do the best you can. Always show people you care." It is a reminder that a leader cannot be arrogant, difficult, and inaccessible and expect that the people who work with them will perform at a high level.

Compassionate leadership is effective leadership

In this book, I demonstrate that leaders who show people that they care about them make the best leaders. If you show people you care, it will make a difference in how they feel about themselves and will improve their performance. Workers who receive compassionate leadership are more engaged and more productive because they work in an environment that inspires them. I have seen this in organizations that are people-focused and people-driven—in organizations that include it not only in their missions and vision statements but work very hard to hardwire it into their cultures. When this approach is authentic and committed, it will permeate an entire organization.

Compassion does not mean hugs and kisses. It means people feel treated with respect. It means you honor and trust the people you lead. People who are treated this way are going to be naturally more engaged and productive. If you just leave them alone and do not support them and recognize them, then they are going to feel like they are not appreciated. They will feel as though they come to work every day to work alone on an island. They do not believe their leader cares about them and their work. And you will have failed them, yourself, and your organization. You'll have failed to be a servant leader. On the flip side, when leaders show their colleagues they care, workers come to work every day with an enthusiasm and eagerness that gives a workplace the kind of life that leads to great things. And, when you get down to the basics of it all, it is as simple as treating the people you lead as human beings.

I know there are probably a few leaders out there who enjoy having conflicts with the people they lead, but fortunately they are rare. Still, too many leaders have these conflicts in their work lives. They dread getting up in the morning to come to work and face the people that work for them. Why? Because they have this acrimonious relationship that often stems from the leader's behavior. Maybe they had a coach or a teacher or a boss who screamed at them all the time, and they think that is what leadership is. That is their model, and they do not know any better. It is a damaging myth that still survives in too many workplaces. It is okay to be upset with someone as a leader, and it is okay to disagree with them. How you manage those moments, though, can speak volumes about you and prove consequential about your success as a leader.

A test of sorts

Before you go any further, I would like for you to answer the following questions that will represent your leadership baseline. At the end of the book, I will ask you to answer the same questions to see if your views changed. You will also be able to compare your end-of-book responses to the responses from leaders who were interviewed for this book. Now, do not peek at the leader results at the end because it is important that your baseline answers and end-of-book responses are not biased by the interviewee results.

Below is the short questionnaire:

1. On a scale of 1-10 with one being the lowest, do you believe that America's workforce feels heard and valued?
2. On a scale of 1-10 with one being the lowest, how engaged do you believe employees and leaders are in their current workplace?

   ♦ **Employees**
   ♦ **Leaders**

3. Rank the following eight values of leading with love and compassion with 1 being the most important:

- **Patience:** mastering the ability publicly and privately to exhibit self-control in challenging and tense situations.
- **Trustful:** encouraging those you lead with support and belief in their talents and skills.
- **Grudgeless:** being willing to forgive professionally and personally.
- **Servant Leadership:** facilitating the success of those you serve leads to both the organization's and your success when you think of yourself less.
- **Walk the Talk:** living and breathing love and compassion values in your daily leadership journey.
- **Honesty:** being open and truthful individually and for anything regarding the organization.
- **Communication:** practicing regular and consistent communication tactics that include genuine encouragement and honest feedback.
- **Commitment:** staying dedicated and true to your personal and professional values no matter what the circumstances—good and bad.

4. What do you believe is the percentage of CEOs nationally that embrace and regularly practice a loving and compassionate style?

Why poor management leads to poor productivity

Why would someone embrace this style of leadership? A July 2019 Gallup survey found that 67 percent of corporate executives are not engaged with their respective organizations. In addition, the same survey found that engaged employees are 44 percent more productive than those who are merely satisfied. Another survey completed in 2013 by Ilya Pozin in the *Huffington Post* listed the ten top reasons people hate their jobs:

10. They think the grass is greener someplace else.

9. Their personal values do not align with the company's.

8. They do not feel valued.

7. They have job insecurity.

6. There is no room for advancement.

5. They are unhappy with their pay.

4. There is too much red tape.

3. They are not being challenged.

2. The passion is gone.

1. They have a terrible boss.

So what do these not-so-encouraging results tell you? First, while pay is always important to one's livelihood, it is rated as only the fifth-worst on the list of reasons people hate their jobs. It is important to note that all of these ten reasons, especially engagement, are primarily driven by leadership. Please also see that the top two reasons people hate their jobs is that their passion is gone, and they have a terrible boss. One can argue that the top two reasons are directly affected by leadership behavior and actions.

The encouraging news is that this book will provide real-life experiences and tools to encourage you to incorporate the eight compassionate values that motivate successful leaders into your leadership style, with the goal of creating a highly engaged workforce that will improve morale and organizational performance. I am excited for you to learn more about this leadership style, and I sincerely hope it will make a positive difference in your leadership life as well as your personal life. Enjoy!

Live the culture and be the culture you want to see.

CHAPTER ONE

PATIENCE

EVERYONE KNOWS THE OLD SAYING, "Patience is a virtue." This is especially true when leading with a loving and compassionate style. Patience is the ability to exhibit self-control publicly and privately in demanding and tense situations. This is a value that is generally undervalued and underappreciated. It is also challenging, especially when leaders are under pressure to produce results faster than anticipated or when results do not meet projected targets.

Never embarrass. Be constructive.

One of the worst things a leader can do is be impatient with someone by admonishing them publicly. How do you think it makes someone feel when they are shamed or embarrassed in front of their peers or, even worse, in front of the colleagues they lead? It will have a negative impact that will linger far beyond the moment in question. At one senior executive meeting, a chief operating officer was questioning one of the other senior executives about customer satisfaction results that recently had slipped, though the executive's organization had consistently met or exceeded targets in the past. The executive responded by saying that extenuating circumstances occurred in the most recent reporting period that may have caused the recent negative results. The COO responded that it was expected that you can "walk and chew gum at the same time" regardless of the stated "extenuating circumstances." This is an example of a lack of patience based on present performance that does not consider past performances. Worse, it involved embarrassing the executive in front of his colleagues.

A bedrock principle of leading with patience is that one should never admonish colleagues in a way that will diminish their personal identity. Thomas Stallkamp, former president of Chrysler Corporation and founder of Collaborative Management, said that it is "okay to get mad at the situation, but not at the people." A well-known historical example, which was depicted in the movie *Gettysburg*, occurred between General Robert E. Lee and Major General J.E.B. Stuart, and emphasizes this point.

When General Stuart failed to complete a key part of his mission and put the Confederate efforts at risk, General Lee could have confronted General Stuart in front of the entire army, or he could have demoted him and diminished his personal worth and identity in front of his fellow officers. What General Lee actually did in the film's telling was invite General Stuart to his private tent, and with firmness and passion, he reminded General Stuart that this type of leadership was unacceptable, and to never let it happen again. General Stuart offered to resign, but General Lee approached him, put his hands on General Stuart's shoulders, and said, "There is another battle coming tomorrow, and we need you. You must take what I have told you and learn from it, as a man does." Do you think General Lee handled this difficult situation that involved men's lives on the battlefield with patience, respect, and care for General Stuart?

In this story, Lee could have made a major issue of Stuart's decisions and wasted time berating Stuart in the pressure-cooker of battle. Many leaders would have. It would have done nothing to help his pursuit or Stuart. He recognized that he needed Stuart to be at his best, so rather than diminishing him, he sought to point out his mistake while preparing his charge for what lay ahead. With the pressure on Lee and the stakes of the moment, the temptation to have lashed into Stuart must have been tremendous.

Practicing patience in a pinch

The challenge of being patient and poised when the pressure is on—when circumstances are tense and you as a leader are in the center of the storm—can be overwhelming. I can acknowledge that though there were times as a leader that I excelled in those situations, there also were times when I did not. When you do not rise to the occasion, you need to be aware of it and learn from it. In the heat of the moment, I learned to stop myself when I felt the urge to lose my composure and to take a deep breath, stop talking, listen to others, sit quietly, and focus on clearing my head. My goal was to lower the temperature in the room and ensure I was thinking clearly rather than being stuck in the muck of emotions.

Sometimes, of course, our colleagues can make practicing patience in a tough moment a demanding task. They may be argumentative and undermining, seemingly intent on pushing your buttons and knocking you off course. This, I feel fortunate to say, did not happen to me very often. When this happens, though, I think of the advice couples in counseling receive when arguments spiral out of control with no end in sight—take a break, step away from the discussion, and then re-engage after some time apart. It is essential to have that courage to stop the discussion when you recognize that a pause is necessary. And when you come back to revive the conversation, it is absolutely critical that it happens face to face, rather than via an exchange of texts or emails.

If tensions arise or a disagreement intensifies in a group setting, maybe an individual interaction would be more appropriate—you should recognize when a discussion would be better managed somewhere other than in front of your team. No leader likes to be attacked or challenged disrespectfully in public. But you have to be true to your principles and values. It is never a good look when a leader fights back and engages in an argument in front of their team. They look to you for strength, and any sign of squabbling will injure that perception. They look to you for patience. They look to you for courage. They look to you for common sense. They do not look to you for pettiness or the kind of weak resolve and loss of control that an argument can suggest to those observing it.

Are there times when you lost your patience and admonished someone publicly? I know that I have made that mistake. One occasion during a very tense meeting with a group of physicians still resonates with me. As a hospital CEO, it is critical to maintain patience no matter how personal the conversations become. Unfortunately, I fell into the trap of losing my composure with a particular physician and lashed out at him with profane and insulting language. This was totally unacceptable behavior from someone who hopes to be a loving and compassionate leader. What could have I done differently to exercise patience with this person? First, I should not have admonished him in front of his colleagues, no matter the circumstance. Second, I should have excused myself from the meeting until I regained my composure and patience. As a result of my impatience, I met with this physician privately and apologized. I also met with the entire group to apologize for my lack of patience and subsequent outburst. It was something that I will never do again.

Mentoring as patient leadership

A great example of leading with patience comes from Gary Paxson, president and CEO of White River Medical Center in Batesville, Arkansas. Mr. Paxson's first mentor also was mentoring Mr. Paxson's colleague who was having challenges in her role. The mentor coached this person in a "loving and patient" style as far as he could, but unfortunately the colleague's employment did not work out, and she was terminated. However, Mr. Paxson's mentor supported her departure with love and dignity by finding her a different role elsewhere.

Another example comes from Richard Caldwell, vice president for Infosys in Indianapolis, Indiana. Mr. Caldwell vividly remembers a senior executive early in his career who consistently modeled patience with him by meeting on many occasions after hours for as long as it took to help guide him to the next level of success.

Mentoring can play a dramatic role in the growth of leaders. The mentoring relationship allows a mentee to speak with a mentor in a confidential, trusting atmosphere about the challenges that they are facing. We have an obligation as servant leaders who walk the talk to help other leaders grow and help other leaders be successful. It is for the good of the organization, but it is also for the good of the world. If those we mentor take their experience and skills to be great leaders elsewhere, then we have succeeded.

Sometimes, in fact, being a good mentor means helping someone change directions and maybe even change professions to find a pursuit that better fits them and makes them happy. Sometimes, your mentee is lost and confused, unsure what they want. Helping them find their way is among the highest forms of servant leadership you can find.

We always need great leaders, and the more of them out there the better for everybody—maybe now more than ever. It is also a fun responsibility and incredibly rewarding. When you watch someone grow as a leader and see the impact that has on their organization—and knowing you played some part in that—their success can feel as satisfying as if it was your own.

I have a mentee who has done amazing work turning around the culture of the organization he leads, and I cannot tell you how much fun it has been to watch his success and the way his confidence level has grown. It only made him hungrier to grow and improve, and we have continued the relationship though he certainly does not need my advice as much anymore. It is always about the in-depth conversations and the eternal search for more wisdom and knowledge. That pursuit is as much of a reward for the mentor as it is for the mentee. We go on that journey together.

Serving as a mentor will make you a better, more thoughtful leader. Answering questions and talking through challenges with others who are eager to become better leaders will help you consider the world of leadership in more depth, and it will inform your own approach to leadership and to the numerous challenges that arise for you on a daily basis. It will force you to be patient and therefore bestow you with the gift of becoming a more patient person.

The power of patient praise

Leading with "patient praise" is another aspect of leading with patience. However, be aware that praise without specifics can be worse than no praise at all. Did you ever experience a leader who walks around every day and tells everyone "good job" or "thanks for a good job" without specifics? After the first ten times hearing this praise, did it still have a positive effect on your performance? Likely not. Diminishing returns accompany praise without specifics because the perception is that the praise is insincere and hollow. A common response an employee may think is: "Heck, everyone hears the same thing, so why should I think I am actually doing a good job and do anything different?"

It is important to remember not to rush to praise or to offer praise without thought. Failing to praise the right way with specifics may create a missed opportunity for improved productivity and morale. Patient praise must be legitimate and concrete, because false praise will likely create credibility issues for the leader and the organization.

An underlying positive here is that specific praise illustrates to others that you are paying actual attention to their work. It is a leader's responsibility to get to know as many people as possible. A key part of that is knowing their work and making sure they are recognized and know that you appreciate the work that they do. When a leader simply praises everyone vaguely, the impression they give is that they do not know what's going on and cannot distinguish good work from mediocre work.

Managing up

Another crucial aspect of patient praise is "managing up" your leaders and colleagues. What exactly does managing up mean? It can be defined as positively supporting others through verbal and nonverbal means, whether you disagree or not with that person. Managing up leads to happiness for the receiving person and that leads to higher morale and likely higher productivity and customer service. The simplest example is when a nurse tells a patient who is going to have open heart surgery that the patient's heart surgeon has outstanding clinical outcomes along with a wonderful bedside manner. That gets the patient in the best possible frame of mind to face what they are about to face.

However, managing up also means that one must be truthful about the person you are managing up.

A CEO at one organization disagreed with the parent company chairman about incentive payments for the leaders of the CEO's company. The CEO's leadership team barely missed their operating margin target because of unanticipated revenue reductions outside of their control. However, this was offset by operating expense reductions that yielded a significant positive under-budget performance that almost made up the revenue shortfall. When it came time to determine incentive payouts, the chairman would not compromise on the rules, which stated that to receive an incentive payout an operating entity must meet or exceed their operating margin target. The CEO disagreed with the chairman's decision and informed him as such. However, despite huge disappointment on the leadership team, the CEO managed up the chairman by stating that he ultimately understood the chairman's position. He understood that he had to be consistent with this guideline throughout the organization and could not make an exception for this leadership team, no matter the extenuating circumstances.

Believe me, it was very difficult for the CEO to face the leadership team and to see the disappointment and sadness on their faces after working so hard to reduce expenses. Managing up can be joyous and uplifting, but also challenging when one disagrees with a decision. Either way, it is the right type of patient praise depending on the appropriateness of the situation.

Practicing patience with yourself

Last parting advice for patient leaders to help ensure success for this value comes from William Geschke, former CEO of a software company in Cleveland, Ohio: "Be patient with everyone, but above all with yourself." That can be immensely challenging advice for a leader to follow. I know it could be for me. The lack of patience we feel as leaders could partly be driven by external pressures. You have targets to hit, metrics to meet, and a supervisor or board watching over your shoulder to make sure you succeed. It can be tough to manage those expectations intellectually and to be patient with yourself, particularly if you have the kind of Type A personality that is so common among leaders. There were times when I couldn't wait and couldn't exhibit the patience that a situation required.

Impatience with yourself and with your inability to bend circumstances to your will—no matter how strong it is—absolutely can affect your leadership if you are unable to manage it. If you are impatient with yourself and with things that you cannot get done, it will create anxiety and worry that will be hard to set aside and that can easily filter to your team. And when you are impatient with yourself, you likely will be impatient with your team and others. Part of the solution is simply trusting your people and providing them the right tools to be successful. The more you do not believe in your people, the more impatient you will be with both them and yourself. Sometimes, you just need to remind yourself that you have the right people with the right understanding of their roles to do the work and then trust them to execute it.

I'll give you an example. When I was leading one hospital, I became frustrated by our reliance on temporary nurses. Temporary nurses travel to different hospitals and fill in gaps where departments are short of the nursing staff required to serve their patients. Temporary nurses are paid more than their permanent counterparts, and that can lead to both budget challenges and morale problems among staff. One reason we needed temporary nurses is because the training process to onboard a new nurse in many departments was so time-consuming and deliberate. This drove me crazy. These were educated nurses with the training necessary for us to hire them, and I couldn't understand why it took them six weeks or even three to six months, depending on the position, to get up to full speed.

I kept asking my chief nursing officer, "So why is this taking so long? I thought they got all this training in nursing school. Why is it that we have to retrain them when they come to our hospital? Why can't they just learn our policies and our procedures, get some training on the floor, and then get to work in a couple of weeks?" My chief nursing officer would get a bit frustrated with me, and she would remind me, "You know, Dave, I have told you this is the process. This is the way it needs to be." She would explain to me again that the extended training period is a necessary step for certain highly technical, highly complex positions.

And, I would slow down and say, "Yes, you are right." She would remind me that the extended training period protected patients and ensured that we were giving them the best possible care. I had gotten frustrated with the situation, and I had grown impatient with my inability to fix it—to limit the use of these costly temporary nurses. The fact was, however, our team was managing the challenge as well as it could, and I needed to recognize that and trust them. I also needed to learn to be patient with myself and come to grips with the fact that I could not solve every challenge our organization faced through sheer resolve. Patience can be a hard thing, but it is necessary. And when you find it and learn to be patient with your team and yourself, it can be rewarding and offer you a clear-headedness that will allow you to view each situation logically—without the emotion that is inherent to impatience.

Takeaways on patience

Final thoughts on the "patient" value of loving and compassionate leadership:

◆ Always praise three times more than admonish.
◆ Never admonish in public no matter how impatient or angry you may feel.
◆ Make every effort to admonish humbly and with compassion.
◆ Patient praise for someone must include specifics for the praise to be effective and sincere.
◆ Manage up a person or situation whenever possible and appropriate, but always manage up truthfully.

CHAPTER TWO

TRUSTFUL

BEING TRUSTFUL WITH THOSE YOU lead can be both rewarding and frightening. Trust is encouraging those we lead with support and belief in their talents and skills. Walter Anderson, a writer, once said, "We are never so vulnerable than when we trust someone—but if we cannot trust, neither can we find love or joy." Do you assume the best and trust the colleagues that you lead or work with? William Geschke told me that he believes in "trusting everyone—until I have reason not to trust them." This is certainly a good place to start when it comes to being a trustful leader.

Open, active listening

What is the number one sign of distrust between a leader and a member of that leader's team? It is interrupting and not actively listening. There are numerous ways of not listening, and some are nonverbal. I recall a time when I entered an executive team meeting as the CEO of a hospital with my mind already made up regarding the elimination of our childbirth program due to financial reasons. My body language included arms crossed, head tilted away from the group, and eyes looking down. I began to ask questions and would answer without waiting for someone else to respond. I was so focused on the financial analysis that I neglected to listen to potential negative outcomes, which included the effect on the community we served. Then, a physician spoke eloquently regarding our hospital's commitment to birthing babies as part of our mission to our community. I finally "woke up" and began to listen, understanding someone else had a better point than I did. We decided to keep birthing babies, because it was the right thing to do for our community and hospital.

Why do leaders not trust those they lead by interrupting them and refusing to listen to them? It is because some leaders think, *My idea is greater than your idea, so I do not have to listen. Interrupting you is okay because your response is not that important. I am not listening to you because I am already preparing my response.* Does this behavior encourage those you lead with support and belief in their talents and skills? Of course not. Instead, those you lead will think: *Why should I say anything to our leadership if they do not take the time to really listen?* This will obviously hinder the future free flow of creative information and new ideas throughout the organization.

You have to create a culture where people do not feel threatened or intimidated—where suggestions are welcomed and considered. People cannot walk on eggshells at work, worried that if they make a mistake they will get fired. That is a culture that does not work. That is a culture that will always underperform because it will never produce the best and brightest ideas. No one can do their best work and their best thinking if they do not feel both heard and safe—if they do not feel trusted.

Trust can be enhanced and supported by actively listening, not interrupting. Below are some helpful suggestions for leaders from Joel Manby's *Love Works: Seven Timeless Principles for Effective Leaders* to help eliminate distrust:

- Avoid saying "I understand how you feel, but …"
- Summarize what you heard. "Okay, I believe I heard you say …"
- Explain the "why" if you decide something different than what was discussed.

Each of these is a good way of demonstrating that you are actually listening and care what your team members say. Remember the number one sign of mistrust is that you do not listen. Listening means actively listening—comprehensive listening. You have to demonstrate that you understand how your team members think and feel when they speak. You have to show empathy for them and what they are telling you. Even if the final decision made for the organization ultimately does not match their thinking or idea, you have to show them that you heard it, considered it, and that it was valued.

Sharing ownership in decision-making

One method for building trust is to listen and involve team members whenever possible in decisions that affect them directly or indirectly. The best decisions are made "with" and not "for." Entrusting others to carry out different aspects of a project or mission both strengthens a team and gives others accountability in the process. John V. Bednar, a retired school principal, started a leadership council that represented all components of the faculty. This leadership team provided input into major decisions affecting the teachers, such as the school calendar, policy and procedure changes, and continuing education. Mr. Bednar always reserved the right to make the final decision, but that happened rarely. Do you think the teachers felt trusted through this model by having input into major decisions that affected their professional and personal lives? Absolutely!

During my career as a healthcare executive and CEO, I started two physician and CEO cabinets. Historically, there has been distrust, sometimes at high levels, between the medical staff and administration in healthcare organizations. To attempt to improve trust and enhance collaboration, my cabinet of medical staff leaders and members would meet to provide input and feedback to the CEO on many topics and issues affecting all involved parties. The only person attending from administration was the CEO to avoid making it appear that this was an "administration-driven agenda." Many difficult topics were discussed that led to improving trust, because the physicians felt that they were really being "heard," with resultant actions. From a selfish perspective, this was my favorite meeting because I learned so much more about them than I would have in other forums, such as traditional medical staff committees. Egos and personal issues were checked at the door and that allowed trust to grow because of open and respectful listening. Will those you lead strive to do their best if they are trusted to be included in the decision-making process? Overall, the answer is a resounding *yes*!

Valuing the consensus

The decision-making process can be a thorny thing. There are leaders who will go through a long group discussion and come to a collective decision on an important issue. Then, later that night or the next day, they will decide that they really did not agree with the decision, and they will unilaterally change it. I strongly recommend that you do not do this unless absolutely necessary. Sometimes, a leader will make this change with new input or new insight that wasn't available at the time of the group discussion, and the change really is for the best of the organization. When this happens, though, you need to follow up with your team and explain what's happening. Too many leaders do not do a good job of explaining the "why" of their decisions, period. That is a dangerous flaw, but particularly when they are reversing the work of a group that has put hard work and thought into the problem at hand.

Some leaders simply view themselves as the decision-makers. They believe they have their title and their salary because they are expected to make these decisions. And that is absolutely true to a point. There are times when that is your job, particularly if you are facing a crisis or a time crunch. You need to have the courage and strength to do that without dawdling or shrinking from the moment. However, when you are making a decision that goes against the grain of your team's thinking, you are doing them and yourself a major disservice by not thoroughly explaining the circumstances and reasoning that led to that change. They do not have to agree with it, but they have to understand where you are coming from. And they have to see that the decision was made with care and with consideration of the care they had already committed to the matter. You owe them a full explanation. Otherwise, their reaction will be to think, "My gosh, we spent all of that time working on that, and we came to a good decision together. And then he just changed it without us. I thought we had a good solution." If you do not provide that explanation, the next time you need their input solving a tricky problem you might find that they are less determined to work through the challenge because they do not see the point. In the end, you'll just decide what you want to decide.

You may be the decision-maker of your team, but you are also the leader—and that means paying appropriate attention to those you lead.

Undermining trust vs. inspiring trust

Trust can be too easily undermined. An example I can share of leadership actions that created high levels of distrust on one team occurred when a CEO set up focus groups of frontline employees without their respective leaders present. The focus group sessions turned into "tell-alls" about managers and led to high levels of distrust between the CEO and leadership team. Even worse, some of the managers were replaced with managers who were not any better, creating disappointment among the employees. A second example is when a CEO was being unresponsive to requests for approval of a matter by a manager. This put the manager in an awkward and tenuous position with their respective teams. The manager then was forced to assume that no answer from the CEO amounted to a *yes*—an obvious strategy to protect the CEO if the manager's decision failed. I am sure you will agree that the trust between the CEO and his leadership team in these examples is probably weak or nonexistent.

Trust can also be developed through how we interact with

one another in different circumstances. The ultimate trusting relationship occurs between a doctor and patient. This relationship is sacred based on the physician's knowledge and plan of care actions for that patient. Just as importantly, the manner in which a doctor interacts with their patient and family members in a genuine and compassionate way enhances and supports that special trust, according to Dr. Kevin Crowe, a cardiologist in West Plains, Missouri.

This is also true when leaders interact directly with their teams. It could be as simple as providing the necessary tools for a housekeeper and then just letting them go do what they do best to provide a clean, safe environment for patients. There are other ways including looking someone in the eye and being truthful when interacting with them. As Richard Flowers recently told me: "Coach, you trusted us enough to provide us the tools and coaching to succeed in practice, which led to numerous personal and team accomplishments." Richard was a team captain on the 1983 Brookside High School Lakeland Conference track and field championship team that I coached. I trusted Richard and the other captains to ensure that all members of the team were completing their practice regimen to the best of their ability by not interfering with their routines.

Micromanagers are ineffective managers

There are micromanagers everywhere. I personally do not believe micromanagers work. I do not think anybody wants to work for a micromanager. I think it creates a level of distrust and some acrimony, because the natural response is to wonder, "Why do you keep telling me what to do? Why do you keep changing what I do?" It is a fine line between a manager providing the appropriate amount of oversight versus micromanaging. It is tough sometimes to understand clearly where that line is, too, because it can greatly depend on the level of skills that the people you lead have.

A leader needs to provide the tools and resources necessary for their teams to be successful without getting in the way. I have always believed that our role as leaders is to facilitate the success of those we lead—to help make it happen rather than making it happen ourselves. That requires much more than saying "good job" every once in a while and much less than closely overseeing every step of your team members' efforts. It is about making sure you provide them the tools to be successful and do their jobs well—in part, by asking them the questions that will ensure you understand what those tools are—and then giving them the freedom, trust, and space to go do it. Organizations that foster a culture of micromanaging also struggle to get anything done. We live in a world that requires rapid responses to the marketplace to get things done in a cost-effective and high-quality way. That is impossible in an organization choked by micromanagement.

I have mentioned my experience as a high school track team coach. I had to oversee that team with just one assistant coach. There were dozens of kids competing in a wide range of events, and there was no way for me to give each one of those athletes anything approaching constant attention. I would write the workouts for them, and they had to go do them. I supervised them as a group. I was out there, providing guidance where I could, but the fact of the matter is that I was trusting them. If they wanted to be better and they wanted to improve and they wanted to be successful, I gave them the tools to do it and then it was up for them to do it. I know they appreciated that trust, and they worked hard in part because of that trust. They wanted to work hard. They wanted to be successful and win a championship. So they took the opportunity and trust I gave them and they ran with it—literally.

As the old saying goes, it is easier to lose trust than to regain trust. To avoid losing trust and to ultimately grow trust, please remember the following:

1. Practice active listening.
2. Do not interrupt.
3. Ensure that you show genuine, open body language when listening.
4. Involve team members in decision-making that has a direct or indirect effect on them.
5. Never undermine a leader.
6. Avoid assuming that your idea is better than someone else's idea.
7. Trust that providing the right tools will lead to individual, group, and organizational success.

It is important to remember that being trustful as a loving and compassionate leader involves being genuine and able to look people in the eye at all times. If you can't look someone in the eye, there usually is a reason for it.

don't communicate with them and do not show appreciation for the information, and then they grow frustrated or leave.

It is about treating people with respect. As a leader, it would be wise of you to remember that your performance depends on the output and productivity of the people you lead. Moreover, they are aware of that fact. If you aren't showing appreciation for their work, you can expect longer-term consequences.

Compensation will always be important to employee satisfaction but communication, the foundation of employee engagement, is more important. You will never be perfect as an organization in this area. Communication has to be coached in so many different ways and modalities. It makes you want to comprehend everything clear. Most of all, though, ... I have talked to CEOs who have in their offices what such that ... was or the issues never got around and talked to people. I am not going to start. They are content to stay in their bubbles and to repeat the mistakes of the past. I really do understand how a leader can be successful if they are not out talking to people and answering ...

Senior managers can be the worst offenders

The following are two eating examples of the kind of poor communication from leadership that can have an unfortunate and uneven impact on an organization — and that can easily be fixed.

I am aware of two different hospital CEOs who kept the doors to their administrative offices locked. If someone wanted to enter the offices, they would either need a special code or to call the desk. Being accessible to communication and on a basic basis about fast-occurring issues is critical for the CEO and the executive team. How would you feel if you were a doctor or employee who

CHAPTER THREE
GRUDGELESS

BEING "GRUDGELESS" AND VULNERABLE MAY be the hardest values for a leader to master because it can be difficult to remove personal emotions from the workplace. How many of you have or are currently holding a grudge against someone at work or in your personal life? As most of us know, it hurts the person holding the grudge in a significant, emotional way. Pastor Jeff Henderson from the Atlanta Buckhead Church said, "The longer you hold a grudge, the longer the grudge has a hold on you." How true that statement is.

The value of vulnerability

Being "grudgeless" means being willing to forgive. This process starts with allowing yourself as a leader to be vulnerable. This can be very challenging for leadership because of the fear of being perceived as "weak." Nationally acclaimed leadership author Craig Groeschel said some of the ways to show vulnerability in a thoughtful way include:

- We may impress people with our strength, but we connect through our weakness.
- Show people what's in your heart and what you value.
- Help people know that you are a loving and compassionate leader.
- Lead with vision, boldness, and vulnerability.
- People would rather follow a leader who is real.

What happens to us does not matter—the only thing that matters is the way we respond. Being vulnerable is the first step in the process toward being "grudgeless." Allen Weiss, former president and CEO of Naples Community Hospital Healthcare System, has the following test for leaders: "Raise your hand if you never made a mistake." Of course, we all make mistakes, but the challenge is when are we willing to admit it to those we lead.

A situation in my CEO career comes to mind. In this instance, communication about terminating a contract with a physician group and hiring another group to provide the same service to the hospital was not handled properly. I had delegated that responsibility to the executive leading the change who then communicated it via email to the outgoing physician group. Needless to say, an angry uproar erupted among the medical staff and some of the hospital board members. I stood in front of the medical staff leadership, the board, and the leadership team to say that the communication should not have occurred this way and that I took full responsibility as the leader of the organization. I allowed myself to be vulnerable to apologize for the miscommunication.

Do you think I could have held a grudge against the executive who put out the inappropriate communication? Absolutely. Was I unhappy with this executive? You bet I was! However, a leader who is willing to be vulnerable and admit mistakes on behalf of the organization as well as himself or herself takes a crucial step toward ending a grudge and forgiving. Have you ever allowed yourself to be vulnerable with those you lead? I hope this chapter will help you feel comfortable doing this going forward.

How does one forgive if the organization you lead has been wronged? Questions to answer when considering action and forgiveness:

- Is it a one-time violation or a repeated occurrence?
- Is the employee self-aware of the violation?
- Are there uncertainties that suggest you should give the offender the benefit of the doubt?
- Will a change benefit the organization and the employee?

The origins of grudges

Sometimes, grudges of a sort can form at the top. Leaders in an organization can develop grudges with each other in the course of the complex and pressure-packed work that they do. Friction develops and personalities clash, likely at the expense of the organization. First of all, that could be a function of the culture of the organization. If leaders feel competitive with each other rather than viewing each other as partners, then the organization is incentivizing success in a way that is counterproductive. However, if you are one of those leaders, you have to recognize that this grudge is a problem for you and your organization. Solving the problem requires a direct but nonconfrontational approach. That means a face-to-face earnest effort to solve the issue with your colleague rather than trying to address things indirectly or via email messages or with passive-aggressive remarks. It will be mutually benefit to you and your colleague. No more meetings and messages tinged with conflict. In fact, your relationship should grow strong from tackling your grudges head-on and together.

Grudges can also form out of ignorance of your colleague and their circumstances. Too often, we are so consumed with our own issues that we do not slow down and recognize that others likely are contending with their own challenges—and often worse ones. When we remain in silos, we lack understanding of others, and that can lead to resentment. Hospitals can be particularly inefficient and insular in this way, though I believe they are getting better.

As a leader, you can help to shine a light on these silent grudges in your teams in a constructive way. Not by forcing people to voice them and causing confrontations, but by working to eliminate the circumstances that allow them to develop and fester. For example, at one of my hospitals we did a survey of the leaders of various departments. The survey attempted to gauge how those leaders rated the service of the other departments in the hospital that they depended on for service or collaboration of some kind. These leaders basically rated the departments as though they were customers. Then, we reviewed the results. For scores that fell below a certain threshold, the leaders involved had to schedule a meeting and develop a plan to address the issues that led to the low score. By design, this was a way of reducing grudges that might be developing through inaction and a lack of communication. And it worked. Processes became more efficient, and lingering issues were addressed.

Another grudge-related challenge that can emerge is someone you supervise working to undermine you or being otherwise disrespectful, either in front of you or behind your back. This is another scenario that cannot be ignored. Someone who looks for opportunities to question your decision-making and generally push back against your leadership can create all kinds of problems, including by infecting their peers and bringing a corrosive negativity to the workplace. Such an employee could sow doubt among others about the direction of the organization and make them question their commitment to the organization.

A compassionate leader caught in this situation cannot let this linger—it will never just go away or solve itself—and the first step is to assess the circumstances and gather information that you can. You want to have a specific, clear understanding of what is happening and not be relying on hearsay and rumors. If it is only innuendo, it is much harder to confront it and solve it. Once you have solid information, then sit down and have a face-to-face discussion with the person. It is a difficult conversation, easier said than done, but it is an important one to have as a compassionate leader. In this conversation, you will be trying to get to the heart of their actions and to build a bridge to them, if possible. You want to understand what is behind their behavior. And then you want to make it crystal clear that we need to be working together and sharing a commitment to the organization.

Disagreements do not have to lead to grudges

Being grudgeless does not mean being a pushover or overlooking the negative impact someone's performance or behavior is having on your organization. It does mean not forming a grudge against that person and allowing it to guide your decision-making.

A crucial belief I have is that disagreements are a necessary part of the decision-making process for an organization. We all spend times in rooms with our colleagues debating knotty challenges, sorting through ranges of solutions, and then forming a consensus around a decision. When that decision is made, it is absolutely essential that everyone in that room gets behind the decision. The debate should be over. If someone still has a disagreement with the decision, they need to have direct conversations about it with the people involved—not disparage it in the hallways and lunchrooms of the workplace. That is how good teams work. I once supervised someone who consistently disregarded this rule. If they disagreed with a decision, they would work against it outside of the conference room, undermining me and the decision with the integral parties involved. We had an initial discussion about this, but the behavior continued. A second discussion followed. When the behavior continued after that, I had no choice but to let him go. Someone that committed to being aligned against an organization can only be a hindrance in the end, spreading discontent and affecting the performance and strength of an organization. To maintain your culture and lower harmful tension, sometimes you have to make that hard decision. You just want to make sure you are making it with a clear head—one not clouded with a grudge.

Remember that a grudge is never really legitimate for a leader to hold in any case, because it affects your ability manage to the best of your ability—grudges truly hurt the person holding them the most. They eat away at you and distract you, and that does nothing to help you or your organization. Great, compassionate leaders have to be willing to forgive both personally and professionally. It may feel natural and tempting to be angry and resentful of someone else—you may even recognize it is wrong and somehow feel borderline powerless to avoid it—but it is never acceptable for a leader to hold a grudge.

The fragile art of dismissal

Letting someone go is one of the hardest decisions you can make. Sometimes, though, it is the courageous decision and necessary to maintaining your authority. Remember that you are not the only one likely bothered by someone undermining leadership and ultimately the organization. It worsens the workplace for the others you lead, too. If you simply look the other way, you will not only harm your standing with others but you will make their work lives less rewarding and enjoyable on a daily basis. Sometimes, when you terminate someone, the people who worked with them will say, "What took you so long?" As a leader, that makes you cringe, because it is a sign that you have not served your entire team as well as you could because you were unwilling to make a difficult, uncomfortable decision. Those words from a worker can feel like an indictment of you as a leader.

A nurse who worked in a surgery department at a hospital I served was found to be stealing narcotic pain medications to support her addiction. This was a classic example of someone who wronged the organization by stealing and, more importantly, put her patients in danger. This was and is a very serious offense at any hospital. After reviewing the facts, it was obvious that she should be terminated. Just before she was to be let go, she asked to speak with me. Most CEOs would be advised not to meet with an employee in this circumstance, but I also had a policy that I would talk to anyone who needed to speak with me if the topic to be discussed was reasonable.

For some reason, I had a feeling that I should meet with her—sometimes leaders have to go with their "gut" when it comes to potentially difficult situations.

At that meeting, she shared with me how remorseful she was and that she fully understood the serious nature of the violation. She was clearly genuine. In addition, she also said that she was desperate to keep her job because of financial hardships facing her family. I looked her in the eye and asked if she was willing to totally give up her drug habit, stay clean, and know that this is the last chance for her at this hospital. Now the skeptics will say that every employee who is facing termination would agree to those requirements. However, I believed she was sincere, and I was willing to forgive her on behalf of the organization and give her a chance at redemption.

To this day, this nurse is still drug free and doing great work taking care of patients. Do all second and even third chances work out for the organization or the employee? In most cases, the answer is *no*. However, is it worth it for the "grudgeless" leader in us to save someone's career and in some cases their lives? Please consider being known more for being slow to fire and quick to forgive than quick to fire and slow to forgive.

Finally, what does being "grudgeless" have to do with being a successful, loving, and compassionate leader? It shows those you lead that you are first and foremost a real human being. Second, it shows that you genuinely care for people.

Third, vulnerability and forgiveness always lead to a positive ripple effect throughout the entire organization. This benefit should never be underestimated. It is important to remember that to be a forgiving leader, one must always act honorably and truthfully to those you lead and serve.

The following is a case study example to consider. A housekeeper was going to be terminated for poor work results along with a negative attitude toward the organization and her job. She also requested to meet with me. I found out that she has faced numerous behavioral health challenges in her past and was currently homeless. I determined that she should be given another chance along with access to behavioral health support. She transferred to another housekeeping position and within a few short weeks, reverted back to her negative attitude toward her work. She wanted more money and more responsibilities than she was capable of handling. It was affecting the morale of her team. What would you now do with this employee as a "grudgeless" leader?

I'll tell you what we did. We told her that this was her job and she needed to treat it with the respect it deserved. If she did not find it acceptable, then she should apply for jobs elsewhere. We gave her a final choice—either continue in her role or leave the organization. Her attitude improved, and she continued in her position.

CHAPTER FOUR

HONESTY AND INTEGRITY

HONESTY, INTEGRITY, AND AUTHENTICITY ARE cornerstone values of a loving and compassionate leader. These values represent the concept of being open and truthful toward both the individuals you lead and toward anything related to your organization. Charles Lindstrom, the late president and CEO of Saint Luke's Health System in Kansas City, once said, "Honesty and integrity is leadership in its highest sense which demands a command of conscience." It asserts itself through commitment and example, rather than through direction.

The need for honesty and integrity for successful leaders is both corporate and individual. In many instances, corporate and individual honesty and integrity overlap, depending on the situation at hand. The leadership challenges for this value include ego, conflict avoidance, weak leadership, and being dishonest from a corporate perspective. It is important to remember that a leader must always be genuine when being honest because most if not all people can tell if they are not hearing the truth.

Humility's link with honesty

Many leaders have a good-sized ego, especially the highly visible and successful ones. It can be a vital piece of strength and an integral component of their abilities as leaders. They sometimes allow their egos to get in the way, often out of fear of harming their standing as a "great leader"—some flawless, imperious creature that does not exist in reality, only in the heads of leaders with inflated egos.

One place where this can be particularly problematic is in the area of honesty and integrity. These kinds of leaders can be reluctant to be honest and risk blemishing the fine public portrait they have painted of themselves. They do not want to admit mistakes, which requires an honesty and self-reflection that they would prefer to avoid. They also do not want to appear weak in front of others, failing to realize that owning mistakes is a sign not only of honesty but of strength. In fact, leaders who cannot acknowledge and face their shortcomings and miscues are by definition weak leaders, lacking the will and resolve to be vulnerable—and therefore appearing all the weaker and more vulnerable for it. If you cannot be honest with yourself, as well as with the people you lead, then you are simply a weak leader.

Some leaders fail the honesty test because of their fear of conflict. They do not speak directly or tell the full truth on a matter because they do not want to tell someone something they do not want to hear and then be confronted about it. They do not want to get stuck in conversations where they do not have the answers—or the answers that someone wants to hear. They do not want to be asked questions that they do not know how to answer.

Corporate honesty

As a leader, you have a fiduciary duty in terms of corporate honesty to provide the most honest information that you can to the people you lead. Now, there are always exceptions. Sometimes, you are working on something highly sensitive that you simply cannot detail at the moment. Perhaps making it widely known would harm the process and jeopardize its success, such as in the case of negotiations or developments of key strategies or efforts. However, those cases still require that leaders are not dishonest or actively misleading, even unintentionally so. You can harm people's trust in you in a way that takes years to repair.

Let us discuss corporate honesty and integrity. Early in my career, I was part of a cutting-edge initiative to align the business goals of cardiologists and cardiac surgeons with the hospital where I worked. The decision was made to enter into a management agreement for the cardiovascular clinical service line with a single cardiology group and to not include the cardiac surgeons and the other cardiology group at the hospital. The negotiations were held secretly until the announcement of the execution of the agreement. What happened next was that the other cardiology group and the cardiac surgeons reacted angrily to the idea that they would be reporting to the managing cardiology group. It created huge amounts of turmoil in the hospital all the way to the boardroom and bred negative morale among the hospital staff members.

Was this an example of corporate honesty and integrity? My answer today is an emphatic *no*. The negative fact that the hospital did not include the other physician groups in the planning and execution of the management agreement was something that took years to overcome. The model actually worked successfully for ten years from a business perspective, but it also led the surgeons and the other cardiology group to leave and set up a new and highly competitive program at our main competitor. It also damaged the integrity and reputation of the executives involved in the process for many years. At a later date, I apologized personally to the physicians who were left out of the management agreement negotiations for my part in this process, which I would classify as corporate dishonesty.

One of the reasons that we held those secret negotiations was because of conflict avoidance. There was a fear that resistance among the cardiac surgeons, especially the leader of the cardiac surgery group, as well as the political dysfunction of the other cardiology group, would stop the plan or project. We were not factually wrong. Afterward, when we announced the deal, both the cardiac surgeons and the cardiology group said they would have done everything they could to stop it. So in some respects, we were right, but it still does not excuse the corporate dishonesty.

And I think we would have been better off just being upfront with them and taking the conflict head-on, even though working through it would have brought major headaches and obstacles to the deal. Finding ways from the outset to include them in the process would have given them the choice to participate or not participate—to collaborate with us or serve as roadblocks—and then they would not have felt as though they did not have a choice after it was announced. I think that is a really good example of corporate dishonesty because it shows when good intentions and pursuit of short-term gain can lead to long-term pain. And it really was at its core about conflict avoidance because we were simply afraid of directly facing the challenge and possibly jeopardizing the project. As I said, you can get so focused on the short-term gains of corporate dishonesty and the benefits to your organization that you miss the long-term effects on the people you lead in terms of trust and confidence in your leadership. In the end, that perceived short-term gain simply evaporates and is forgotten while the long-term consequences are carried forward.

Some guidelines to follow for corporate honesty and integrity to remember when interacting with other leaders and employees:

- Do not shoot the messenger. We all know what that means, and we have all encountered the downsides of overlooking this rule in the workplace. If somebody comes to a meeting with difficult or sensitive information—or just plain bad news—as human beings, we have a tendency to blame the messenger for the information. And, of course, that is the opposite of what they deserve for providing an honest report. Blaming them only ensures that they and their colleagues will be less likely to provide honest information in the future, leaving you and your team in the dark.

- "Fuss and discuss," as described by Joel Manby, author of *Love Works*. Everybody should have the opportunity to speak openly about a topic without repercussions and get their feelings and concerns out on the table for discussion in the interest of an honest conversation that leads to the best possible solutions.

- Ensure that everyone has an opportunity to provide their honest perspective. As a leader in discussions, you should be aware of who is talking and who is not. If someone is not contributing, the reason could be that they simply do not have anything to say. But it could be that they have a reluctance to speak for other reasons—the tone of the conversation perhaps or an opinion that cuts against the grain—and you want to work to create an environment where they feel more comfortable sharing their thoughts. It is okay, for instance, to call on them, almost as though you are a teacher. Let them know explicitly that you are interested in their perspective. That can be the entry point they need, especially if the conversation has a competitive edge and they are disinclined to maneuver for attention. You do not want to miss the insight that leads to the best decision because a team member decided not to speak up.

- Speak now or forever hold your peace. A well-worn, favorite saying for a reason. As I have mentioned, some leaders will walk out of a room after a group has come to a decision, and then continue the debate in the hallway or the parking lot and alter the decision. That undermines the discussion and the corporate honesty of the decision-making process. I encouraged open and honest dialogue "in the room," but once a decision was made and we walked out of the room we were all accountable for the decision. Unified, responsible to each other for "holding our peace" and not second-guessing the decision, thereby weakening it.

- Leader always speaks last. Sometimes, leaders—and I include myself here—are so anxious to get our point out into the world, the one we have been pondering in the lead up to a meeting, that we kick off the discussion with our take on the right answer in a way that can feel pre-emptive, tamping down dissenting views and precluding a productive, honest discussion. The atmosphere immediately goes from collaborative to hierarchical. It is so important for the leader to ensure that everyone in the group has an opportunity to give their honest perspective—to fuss and discuss—without the leader overwhelming the discussion. It also ensures that a leader does not jump to a decision without considering all of the viewpoints. If the leader waits to weigh in last, they can take careful consideration of the points that have been made, demonstrate to their team that they have actively listened, and then help to narrow in on a decision that makes sense. This decision likely will not please everyone in the room, but at least it will consider them—and demonstrate to them that that consideration is authentic.

These are applicable when discussing complicated and sensitive topics related to the organization. When discussing these issues, especially related to business metrics, are you honest about the organizational challenges to meet these metrics? This is particularly true when sharing financial data. It is vitally important that all participants, whether it is at executive-level meetings or when presenting at employee forums, be honest about the direction of the organization and the challenges ahead. How do leaders expect employees to support required changes to survive and thrive if they do not know the facts? You will experience amazingly positive results after being genuine and authentic. Putting it another way,

I would rather "overshare" when it comes to corporate honesty, as long as the truth does not jeopardize the organization.

The temptations and hidden traps of corporate dishonesty

One of the challenges someone in a major leadership position may face is the temptation to be less than honest in the corporate sense with employees. Why? Let us be realistic, the concern is jeopardizing one's credibility with executive leadership and even worse, one's personal employment and career with their company. The first step would be to have a direct conversation regarding your concern with your direct report, or the board if you are the CEO, to determine if your corporate honesty philosophy is a fit with the corporate honesty policy of the organization you serve. At that point, you have a decision to make regarding your continued employment with your organization.

Why can corporate dishonesty be seen as damaging? It is a dilemma for some leaders, because the temptation to go down that road can be so strong, especially in the midst of the daily pressures and complexities of helping to run an organization. Nobody likes being the leader with the bad news, and it can seem so easy to put delivering that news off until another day. The big problem, of course, is that you keep putting it off until it is too late and the damage is done. If things are not going well with an organization—if you are navigating a period of crisis—then it feels devastating to pile bad news on top of bad news. Leaders can yield to the temptation to decide to not be fully honest and soften the blow, suggesting things are not really as bad as they are. Or they exaggerate their optimism for the future and the impact of new initiatives to bolster the organization. People will justify this to themselves as trying to keep the team's spirits up and being positive and inspirational or encouraging buy-in to the organization's newest efforts. You should recognize the detrimental impact this will have on your relationship with your employees, as well as the ways that it should run counter to your moral compass.

Corporate dishonesty can also occur in ways that are not expected—and, in fact, are unintentional. In one of my first manager positions, I was excited to offer an in-house training program to help electrocardiogram (ECG) technicians grow into a higher-level position with better compensation. What I did not realize from a corporate honesty perspective was that since the ECG technicians were members of a bargaining unit, I needed to secure the approval of the union for the program before implementation. Subsequently, the union filed a grievance to stop the program. Sadly, the advancement program did not occur, which was unfortunate for the technicians. Would the program have been successfully implemented had I gone through the correct corporate honesty process with the union? Odds are yes because I believe their problem was not with the program but with the process. It is a reminder that the process—and whether it is perceived as honest—can dramatically affect how a decision or initiative is perceived. Effectively, the perception of dishonesty can undermine your best ideas.

That was a great life lesson for me. The experience occurred in one of my earliest management positions, and I was gung-ho to do something positive for these employees—to make a difference both for the organization and for their careers. It was a diverse group of employees, and collectively they had expressed a strong desire to grow and develop their skills. Being the young, ambitious leader that I was, I was quick to charge forward without awareness of the technical steps that needed to be included because of their membership in bargaining units. The result was that it appeared that I was trying to run an end around on the union, when I had simply been ignorant of the required process and eager to help these workers.

The perception of corporate dishonesty, even when that was not the intent, will create limitations in the development and openness of new ideas and concepts. If employees believe that the leader has been dishonest with them, it affects their own commitment to honesty. It creates a culture and environment that does not support and promote open dialogue between leaders and the people they lead.

Honesty with underperforming employees

We are all aware of the importance of individual honesty and integrity in our personal and professional lives. It seems that everything about us as a human being revolves around our honesty and integrity. This is also true when reviewing an employee's performance. It is a common mistake during these discussions to not be fully honest for fear of a confrontation. Ann Stallkamp, former hospital board member at McLaren Northern Michigan, said, "The dilemma of being loyal to a key member of your group when that person can no longer give value to the organization is a regular challenge. Is this person able to be coached up to be a more productive member of the team, or should they be asked to step aside in an honest way?" This clearly requires an open and transparent conversation with that employee.

Can someone be terminated through honest communication while still protecting that person's dignity? How? The following are suggestions to follow during the anxious and sometimes nerve-wracking firing process.

Ensuring that the employee fully understands their performance issues before termination is the only remaining solution. Are you willing to provide an honest and reasonable plan for the employee to receive a second chance or maybe even a third chance?

Can you present and communicate this plan in a private, dignified manner? It is important that the conversation occur in a very private location, so as to not embarrass or humiliate the employee. Please remember that terminations that become public have a negative ripple effect across the organization toward management.

Support the termination with an offer of transition. Corazon, a clinical service line consulting firm that was recognized as one of the top workplaces in the healthcare industry for 2020 by *Modern Healthcare*, offers a six-week transition for employees to look for another job in addition to some form of severance, depending on the circumstances of the termination.

Be gracious, humble, and compassionate. For the terminated person, they are about to enter a terrifying time in their life both professionally and personally. Being gracious, humble, and compassionate at this time is just the absolute right thing to do. In addition, I would advise you to never arrange for the escort of a terminated employee from an organization accompanied by security, unless there is the threat of violence or breaking the law. Security walking someone out of the building may lead to increased tension and anger among the employees left behind.

Based on what I have heard and seen over my career, I know that most dismissal conversations are not handled well. A big part of that is that they are very hard to do. Honesty plays a big part in that. We have an obligation as leaders to be as honest as possible for this human being, but in as kind and compassionate a way as we can. In many cases, it turns into a very acrimonious discussion. Now, part of that is because of the person that is being dismissed, especially if they are totally surprised by it. You have to have your facts in front of you and give them the honest reasons for their dismissal. That can be done without being cruel or inhumane.

Leaders who dismiss employees without dignity risk upsetting those workers who remain, too. They often will remain friends with their old colleagues, and news of their treatment will spread rapidly through an organization. The negative ripple effects will have people saying, "Hey, if this person gets treated like that, what's going to keep me from being treated the same way?" It creates a lingering negative perception of the organization and you that is hard to get rid of. And it can be avoided with honesty.

Sometimes, in fact, trying to soften the blow for the employee— being dishonest to try to make them feel better—will backfire. When you praise someone for being a good worker or a hard worker when they were not, you are not doing them any favors and you are also building a case against your decision to dismiss them. Those mixed messages will undermine you and your message to them. You have to stick to the facts of the dismissal. It will be better for both the employee and the organization in the long run, even if it makes the conversation more difficult in the moment. If it is done in a dignified, honest manner, it will have a positive ripple effect in the organization because people will understand. In addition, honest, compassionate feedback to the person being dismissed will help them see clearly the reason for losing their job and help them in their future endeavors.

Be open to honest feedback about yourself in this process. Listen closely and avoid reacting defensively to words from the affected employee.

How many of you start potential coaching or termination discussions with the following: "You did a great job on the project along with being a hard worker." Then the conversation turns to "But ..."

Is this not a mixed message? I was coaching an executive regarding her repeatedly undermining our organization and my work in particular. I made the mistake of starting the conversation reviewing the good results her division was producing for the organization. I then asked her about the incidents of undermining, and she was very surprised and wondered why she was not made aware of this accusation sooner. Was I sending her mixed messages? Yes, which made the rest of conversation extremely difficult. Unfortunately, it ended with her termination. My takeaway learning point was that I was not individually honest with her prior to the conversation.

This could have been avoided if the following individual honesty process was followed both for coaching and performance reviews. This model was developed and followed successfully by Joel Manby as outlined in his book, *Love Works*. Manby suggests the following for starting coaching and performance review conversations:

- Same as—Remind employee to keep doing the work the same as now if results are good. Praise can be included.
- More of—Results and outcomes need to be achieved at a higher level.
- Less of—Lower than expected results or undesired behavior.

This model allows for individual honesty to occur that encompasses appreciation for current work, issuing challenges for even better results, and ends with a plan to do "less of" unacceptable results and behaviors.

No corporate honesty without leadership honesty

Dr. Kevin Crowe, a cardiologist, said, "A leadership style that is honest, genuine, and full of integrity can increase employee engagement and organizational performance, but it must be sincere for this to work and will take time and effort by leadership." It is clearly worth the effort to follow the steps outlined in this chapter for individual and corporate honesty and integrity for the benefit of the organization and ourselves. As the old saying goes, "All we really have is our integrity."

I have talked a lot about the detriments of various forms of dishonesty, and one thing to remember is that your organization will reflect your leadership. If an organization's leaders are less than honest in their interactions, if that is the model that they establish, then you absolutely can count on the organization following that lead. If a leader is dishonest, then how can they expect the people they lead to be honest in their actions and behaviors. On the flip side, of course, a leader who acts with honesty can set the tone for an entire organization. If you extol the benefits of honesty and integrity, and walk the talk in your behavior, then employees will respond accordingly. This goes beyond the simple fact that being honest is just the right thing to do.

Here is a scenario to consider: a trusted leader deliberately makes the decision not to participate in a strategic quality improvement project developed after many agreed-upon discussions among the executive team. This person's excuse was that he did not have the time because of other demands and that he did not trust some of his executive team colleagues. He also developed a "they" attitude toward the corporate team with his employees because he disagreed with the decision. At this point, it is time for the honest "same as," "more of," and "less of" model discussion between the CEO and this executive. Some examples of the "same as" topics in the discussion could include: your work ethic is endless, and you are proactive. "More of" could include advising they use more examples of teamwork when discussing the corporate team with his employees, and "less of" could address his venting to third parties with negative energy and not fully supporting the decisions of the executive team.

What else would you consider including in this important, honest conversation?

CHAPTER FIVE

COMMUNICATION

COMMUNICATION MAY BE THE MOST important value of a loving and compassionate leader. Unsurprisingly, poor or inadequate communication is often rated by team members and employees as a strong indicator of low job satisfaction. Timely, honest, and transparent communication could be the number one challenge to increasing employee engagement. Why? This chapter will explore why so many leaders fail to communicate adequately. Then, it will provide easy-to-implement methods for improving communication.

Why respect is required

People really do love to be appreciated. Money is important, but money has its limits as a reward for many people. Most of us need something more. You can pay somebody more money but if you do not communicate with them and do not show appreciation for the job that they do, then the "glow" from the money will fade. It is about treating people with respect. As a leader, it would be wise of you to remember that your performance depends on the output and productivity of the people you lead. To be sure, they are aware of that fact. If you are not showing appreciation for their work, you can expect long-term consequences.

Compensation will always be important to employee satisfaction, but communication—the foundation of employee engagement—is more important. You will never be perfect as an organization in this area. Communication has to be attacked in so many different ways and modalities. It must be constant, comprehensive, and clear. Most of all, though, it has to be a priority. I have talked to CEOs who stay in their offices who say, "Well, my predecessors never got out and talked to people. I am not going to start." They are content to stay in their bubbles and repeat the mistakes of the past. I really do not understand how a leader can be successful if they are not out talking to people.

Senior managers can be the worst offenders

The following are two telling examples of the kind of poor communication from leadership that can have an unfortunate, significant impact on an organization—and that can easily be fixed.

I am aware of two different hospital CEOs who kept the doors to their administration offices locked. If someone wanted to enter the offices, they would either need a special code or to call the desk. Being accessible to communicate on a timely basis about fast-occurring issues is critical for the CEO and the executive team. How would you feel if you were a doctor or employee who needed to urgently talk to someone in the executive offices? Do you think this type of communication, nonverbal but powerful and symbolic, leads to mistrust and miscommunication? Would it make you feel valued? The implication, of course, is that you are not welcome and neither are your ideas and insight.

I was told that senior management at one large manufacturer very rarely came to the floor to talk to the line employees. These employees would get adequate updates from their floor management supervisors, but they never heard from senior management when it came to recognition for accomplishments or to recognize them for doing something right. There were very few "thank you" messages and very little support or acknowledgement. All they cared about were production quotas. This lack of communication clearly was very disappointing for the floor-line workers. Lack of specific and targeted recognition communication from senior management, whether it is verbal or nonverbal, sends a message to frontline employees that their performance is not important unless something negative occurs. It also shows a lack of respect for employees and their performance.

Senior managers often are the worst offenders in organizations. They react and communicate to negative moments, but remain distant and silent when team members excel and thrive. It is disrespectful to the employees working there. It is obviously important to be clear and direct, and direct conversations are essential when a team falls short of goals or makes a consequential mistake. However, direct conversations are also just as essential—and I emphasize the word essential here—when teams exceed expectations. Or when they encounter a difficult challenge and excel in the face of it. If you are a leader and want to see those results, then you need to demonstrate that they mean something to you and the organization. That is an important way that organizations achieve higher levels of excellence.

The value of vulnerability

The above examples happen too frequently. One reason for this is that there are leaders who are not comfortable interacting directly with employees, in person or even sometimes in writing, for fear of being questioned and not being able to answer those questions, or of having some type of negative confrontation and saying the wrong thing. I believe these leaders feel this way because they are worried about possibly "looking bad" or weak as a leader. Overcoming this concern is difficult, but it is an essential step for a leader to take. It involves forming a willingness to not take criticism personally and to becoming open to admitting when you are wrong. It is amazing how positively employees react when leaders admit their mistakes.

There are leaders who do not communicate well due to a fear of vulnerability. It is easy to send emails. It is easy to send texts. It is easy to send memos. But having face-to-face conversations can be another matter for some people, especially if they are afraid of personal criticism or not being able to answer questions that they are asked. Believe me, I have encountered more than one leader—someone who by the nature of their job is accustomed to pressure and stress—lose their temper because they got caught flat-footed in front of other people. Nobody likes to be embarrassed, but a fear of embarrassment will prevent you from ever being a truly effective leader—not to mention the ways it will hamper your growth as a person.

Learning to be comfortable communicating

One way to navigate these waters with more confidence is to establish ground rules or processes that can help you be more comfortable in these situations while limiting the types of interactions that you would be keen to avoid. For me, I loved speaking with members of the employee population, even if there was a risk of some type of criticism. I always figured occasional criticism is a necessary price to pay for the opportunity to serve in a leadership position. It can be unpleasant and uncomfortable, even when the criticism is delivered in a constructive way. However, I made it clear that respectful criticism was completely acceptable to me. In fact, it can serve as a vital source of information to you, making you better at your job and strengthening your organization, as long as you receive it in the proper spirit and view it in a productive light.

Once you learn to set aside the instinct to take it personally, it can feel powerful to be open to criticism and complaints. How do you get to that point? Practice. You need to face the music over and over again until you grow the thick skin you need and gain the confidence that is necessary to put yourself in that situation. Learning by doing, as simple as that. Also, be prepared. Prepare and prepare and prepare. That way you are more likely to have the answers you need if the questions get tough. If you are surprised, there is no reason to panic. Remember that you do not have to have all of the answers on the spot. No one can pull that off.

Still, I made it clear that I simply would not continue the conversation if the conversation crossed a line and became disrespectful. There is no reason to accommodate someone who communicates that way. Taking a stand on that is in line with the well-known wisdom that you teach people how to treat you.

If you want to be a compassionate leader, then you have to learn to be enthusiastic about interacting personally with those you lead. One of the prerequisites to being a compassionate leader is liking people. If you do not like people, then quite frankly you should not be leading them. You need people to get things done. You can be a wizard on the income statements and balance sheets and maybe even strategies and growth, but if you cannot communicate with the people you lead—the people you ultimately depend on for success—then you are not going to be successful. In my experience, people often are simply happy to have the opportunity to speak with you, share their experiences and insight, and they prefer to be polite.

I shared earlier in the book about the time when the financial performance of the organization I was leading was not going to achieve its operating margin target because of revenue shortfalls that were out of the leadership team's control. I assured the team members that if they significantly reduced their expenses below budget, that I could get them at least part of their annual bonus. Unfortunately, corporate leadership did not approve my request for an exception for a bonus.

I faced the leadership team and told them that I was wrong for implying that the bonus policy would be modified for not achieving their operating margin target. The hardest part about being vulnerable for me that day was seeing the looks of disappointment and sadness in their faces as I communicated to them in person that there would be no bonus even though they performed admirably on my request to reduce expenses. While hard to communicate and difficult to hear for the audience when a leader is wrong, it is important as a loving and compassionate leader to communicate truthfully and transparently to maintain credibility, and more importantly, because it is the ethical thing to do.

Knowledge should be shared

Many leaders do not understand or know how to use different methods of effective communication. Some simply do not want to take the time required to provide effective communication. Others construe possessing knowledge as power and the more information shared with others then the less power they believe they possess. This is obviously unethical and unprofessional because it will undermine an organization's performance and ultimately its chance at being successful. It is a sign of a leader who is more invested in their personal standing than in the success of their organization and its employees.

Still, there are some leaders whose ego tricks them into believing that hoarding knowledge is a form of power. I have heard of CEOs who deliberately keep their executive teams uninformed and in the dark on certain key matters. Unsurprisingly, these are the same leaders who tend to hog the spotlight and grab as much glory for themselves for any successes as they can.

These leaders largely will manage to inspire only resentment in the people they lead. If they are hoarding knowledge to attempt to keep people they lead dependent on them, they will soon learn that they have accomplished the opposite and encouraged similarly selfish behavior that could cause problems for them and the organization. Soon, they will not be the only people hoarding knowledge, and they'll find that the flow of new information slows to their office—and they are every bit as in the dark as those they lead, if not more so. It is yet another reason that selfish leadership is not effective leadership, and another way that ego can serve as a formidable obstacle to success. Trusting others and sharing the knowledge you have is where real, effective leadership lies.

Effective formal modes of communication

There are many successful ways that leaders can communicate company updates and business in a positive and transparent fashion. The first and most obvious way is to hold regular town hall meetings for all employees. A requirement for me as a CEO was to hold quarterly town halls. These town halls would have numerous sessions to ensure all employees had an opportunity to attend one. There was usually a fun theme, as well as a question-and-answer session at the end. I would do my best to answer every question honestly and factually, but I also had a rule that the person asking must be respectful to the organization and me. I did not answer questions that included attacks on me or the organization. I cannot emphasize enough the importance of these town halls because everyone wants to see and hear from the CEO about how the company is performing. Town halls can be virtual as well, although they may not be as effective as in-person meetings.

There are the usual communication methods to practice such as newsletters and departmental or work group meetings. These are required and should be vigorously supported. Direct contact from leaders in formats such as emails and videos can have an enduring impact. I can tell you that employees are very appreciative of it, and that leads to higher engagement. An employee from McLaren Northern Michigan hospital, where I served as the president and CEO before retiring, told me, "I wanted to thank you especially for the daily communication emails. I have worked other places (even much smaller places) where I never heard from my own supervisor let alone the CEO of the company. Communication is one of the things I value most in a workplace, and I really appreciate the regular effort by you to reach out to encourage and make us laugh and make everyone feel a part of the team." Do you think this employee will perform at a higher level because she has a better understanding of what is going on within the organization thanks to this style of communication? Similarly, Thomas Stallkamp, former president of Chrysler Corporation and founder of Collaborative Management, said he sent weekly video messages to company employees stressing speed, innovation, and performance while emphasizing employee involvement as the key to Baxter's success. Do you think this made a difference in Baxter's performance as a company? I do.

Here are some practical things you can do to improve communication to the entire employee population, making it personal and transparent. The first suggestion is to send daily emails. Why not take advantage of technology to connect individually with each employee? In each daily email message to my staff, I included an inspirational quote, positive encouragement, organizational "wins," any relevant hospital news, and finally a corny joke. Yes, a corny joke was included to add a little humor for someone who may be working in a very stressful environment that day. Many times, employees would send me quotes and jokes to share. I happily included their submissions and then credited them on that day's email message. I believe this communication tactic was very successful as evidenced by an increase in organizational employee engagement scores each year.

Most importantly, I as the CEO felt a unique connection with everyone on a daily basis. I received many comments and "thank yous" for both the inspirational messages and the jokes. One employee said, "I have not met you in person but have felt connected to the McLaren Northern Michigan family via your daily message." Another comment: "You are a very hands-on CEO which I am sure is very appreciated, and I have enjoyed reading your daily emails." Finally, a colleague wrote that "I have thoroughly enjoyed your emails of inspiration and chuckles. I respect the fact that you feel it is important for all colleagues to know what is going on in the organization. You have encouraged a culture of communication and one that respects and values the work of each colleague. Your positive attitude is infectious, and I have great respect for you!" I hope you will try a daily email message that is short, positive, and informational and that can be read in thirty seconds by all of your valued employees.

Another simple recommendation is writing personal thank you notes. Writing personal thank you notes is a way to show the organization cares. The thank you note should be handwritten and sent to the employee's home. Many times, the employee's family is thrilled to receive the note from the CEO. Sometimes they even put it on their home refrigerator with all of the children and grandchildren notes! Also, many employees proudly hang their thank you notes up in their office. The CEO needs to ask their leaders to send them names of those in their departments or groups who should get a thank you note. The CEO should copy the leader of the employee's department on the thank you note so as to manage up the leader who made the recommendation. After one note I sent to an employee, they wrote: "Thank you for being a person of excellence and for setting a good tone for our organization. I will always remember your handwritten thank you note to me. You are right, in that it means more than you know!"

Accessibility and informal communication

Accessibility is an overlooked component of communication. I believe the most important and effective way to communicate is person to person. This does take time, but not as much as one would think. Everyone says their "door is always open," but realistically, is it for you? I had a rule that my door would always be open unless I was in a meeting that required privacy. I welcomed employees that wanted to talk with me for a minute or just say "hello" as they were walking by. Many times, they had questions about something related to the organization that I was happy to answer if I could.

At Ozarks Medical Center in West Plains, Missouri, where I served as the president and CEO, my office had two doors. One was to the executive suite and the other was to the hallway on the way to the cafeteria. There were many occasions when I left the hallway door open and employees stopped by to just say hello or chat for a few minutes. Do you think these employees felt more engaged with the organization because they were comfortable talking to the CEO? The lesson here is that if you are willing to provide the time, then accessibility is a tactic to improve morale and engagement, and more importantly, it is fun getting to know the good folks that work in your organization.

I met a man at a church group soon after I retired who asked me what I had done in my career. I told him that I had been the CEO of a hospital.

"Oh, my gosh," he said. "And you are talking to me?"

"What do you mean?" I asked.

"I worked for a trucking company for years," he said. "I drove a delivery truck. I was never allowed to speak to the CEO. You just did not do that."

His response spoke volumes to me about his previous work environment, and it also made me think about how disappointed I would be if I ever heard of an employee of an organization that I had led saying something similar. Some CEOs and executives want to appear above the fray, floating above the daily doings of the people they lead. What a mistake that is. Accessibility and approachability are necessary to good leadership. I am absolutely convinced of this truth. The more inaccessible you are to your employees, the more removed you are not only from the operations of your organization but from understanding the strengths and weakness of your organization. And how can you lead what you do not actually understand?

The art of walking around

Other accessibility tactics to consider are having informal coffees and lunches with employees and taking time for formal and informal "walking around," a term used by Philip Weintraub, Special Assistant to the Vice Chairman of the Board of Governors of the Federal Reserve System. Admittedly, taking the time for "walking around" was challenging for me. It is an easy thing to leave off a busy schedule—something you put on your calendar with the best of intentions, only to strike it to catch up on your emails or polish a speech you've got to give to the Rotary Club. However, it is so important for you as a leader to walk through your staff's work areas and maintain a regular presence. In addition, it is important to be prepared to hear things you may not like or want to hear. Walking around will fail as a communication strategy if a leader does not listen and does not provide follow up through the manager of that area. It is critical that the CEO or executive not undermine the department leader but instead work with that leader to address the employee's concerns while managing up the leader. Walking around can be a bit dangerous if you are not comfortable talking to employees, but this is another excellent communication opportunity.

I know that walking-and-talking is one of those ideas that can seem great in theory and difficult and unproductive in practice. It is not as simple as just getting out and about and being seen. People will appreciate you visiting them in their workspace only if you show a genuine interest in what they are doing and ask the kinds of questions that reflect that level of interest. Too many leaders swing by an office or cubicle, offer an inauthentic "How's it going today?" with a fake smile, nod politely and distantly at the reply and then move onto the next worker, as though they were simply checking boxes or meeting a quota that reduces each worker to a metric. You might as well stay in your office if that is the approach you are going to take. Everyone you encounter will form a crystallized vision of you as the detached boss speaking from a script and not bothering to pay attention to the answers they get from their questions.

In fact, you can work from a sort of script without sounding scripted if you put in the effort. First, make sure that the worker is not swamped with work, and you are not arriving at a difficult time for them to look up from their tasks. Do not just assume that it is a good time for them to speak with you. Be clear that you do not want to slow them down but wanted to see if they had a moment to talk. Develop basic questions that you ask to get someone talking. What are you working on today? Is there anything I can do to help you with your job? Where do you think our organization is falling short these days? How can we improve? Tailor them to their work responsibilities as best as you can. Listen carefully to what you hear and respond with questions to generate a genuine discussion.

It sounds so simple, but so many leaders do not make the minimal effort to do it. One great conversation is worth much more than a dozen conversations done for nothing more than show. If that means you only talk to a single employee during your sojourn to "manage and walk," it will be well worth it. The conversation could prove pointed if the employee has an issue that is really bothering them, but that information can prove valuable because it tells you something about your organization that you never would have heard in your routine meetings.

Leaders should do everything possible to get to know the employees they lead as people. This does not mean invading their privacy, but it is important to learn as many first names as possible. When you learn about a family concern or a family accomplishment, ask the employee about it. Examples include children's accomplishments, family illnesses, or other hardships. I will never forget the appreciation on the face of a leader on my team when I told her that her five-year-old son who had cancer was in my thoughts and prayers. I continued to ask her about his progress every time I saw her. Likewise, I followed another employee's son who was a star athlete at the local high school. You could see the delight in her face when I talked to her about his achievements in his last game. Again, get to know your employees because it is the right thing to do, but it will also support your informal communication and, most importantly, increase employee engagement because it will show you genuinely care about them and their families.

When walking around as a leadership communication tactic, there is another guideline—it is important to professionally and cheerfully great every employee you encounter. It is imperative to follow the 10 and 5 Rule, which is to smile at someone you encounter ten feet away and address someone with a "hello" who is five feet away. This sounds so basic, but it is amazing how this rule—a mainstay of the hospitality industry—is not followed by leaders. And that cascades down throughout the organization. I was at a major academic medical center for an appointment with my granddaughter and not a single person said hello to us as we walked down the hallways. In fact, most of them had their heads down. They certainly did not follow the 10 and 5 Rule. The message here is that leadership at this particular academic medical center probably does not follow this value either, since it appears the employees are not following the rule. Remember what Victor Borge said: "A smile is the shortest distance between two people."

Following through with purpose

And remember that closing the loop with the employee is essential. If you get questions that you cannot answer in the moment, you cannot just tell the person you'll get back to them—you have to actually do it. Otherwise, you'll build yourself a reputation as the executive who does not listen and does not follow through. Managing up is one ideal way to follow through. That means connecting with the employee's manager to get the answers and get the answers back to the employee. For instance, I would walk into the laundry and have conversations with the workers there. They would ask me questions about the organization or their jobs, and I would answer them when I could. When I did not have answers ready, I would promise someone would get back to them—making it clear that it might be someone else in the organization—and then connect with their supervisor to collaborate on getting them a response on our behalf. It is important to keep their manager in the loop so that they are aware of their employees' concerns and questions so that you do not undermine that manager in some way, either in reality or in perception.

Following through can be powerful for the people you are helping. They recognize that you are interested in their work and value it enough to devote your own time, energy, and focus to it. Not following through simply shows them the opposite. That is why closing the loop is a mandated component of visiting with employees. You do not want to sound like the stereotypical politician responding to every tough question with, "I'll have to circle back with you on that," when they really mean, "I am never going to answer that question." That is not leadership by any definition.

That extra step—the follow up—is absolutely a challenge for the executive who stops by offices to visit and check in. It can be a lot to keep track of, and they are already very busy people. It is almost like being penalized for taking that time out of their day to do something they do not need to do. However, if the visiting part is all you ever do, then why bother? Nothing changes for the employee, and no progress or growth results from it.

Why mere conversations matter

I saw firsthand how often these conversations meant something to the employees. Often, they did not have major issues they wanted to discuss. They just wanted to talk about their lives, and those conversations were worthwhile, too. They were a great way to get to know as many employees as possible and to show interest in them. Sometimes, I had learned about something that had happened in their lives from a supervisor or someone else, and I would ask about it, doing my best not to be intrusive but to show support. I always asked if there was anything that we could do for them. Often, they just appreciated the opportunity to talk to someone about it.

Remember that these conversations, in the end, are every bit as important for you as they are for the people you are seeking out. When you are an executive, most of the information that reaches you has been diluted. It has been filtered through multiple layers and has taken on a shape that is likely very different than its original form. Smart CEOs and executives will have as many conversations as they can with people closer to the front lines.

You might remember the TV program *Undercover Boss*. The premise of the show was that a CEO would disguise themselves and work in a low-level position at the company they operated. Part of the audience appeal of the show might have been the idea that the boss would uncover something untoward in their operations, and a big part certainly was the fun of seeing "a suit" getting their hands dirty with the types of tasks they were not used to filling their days doing. The most striking part of the show, though, was how much the CEOs learned every time about their operations. They found out valuable information about the people they lead and what they face every day. That kind of information is golden to a leader, and they will never be able to learn it sitting in their offices.

If this is a part of the job that you are reluctant to do, know that you could be missing out on something that will invigorate you and make you love your job more. I love learning about people. So many people leave the workplace and live such different lives away from work. Sometimes, those lives are very difficult. In some cases, you might be able to provide them some concrete help—provide some guidance or even point them to company resources that can help. For instance, I spoke to an employee who was struggling to get answers about health insurance support for some restorative surgery that she needed. Our plan was self-funded, and she couldn't get any answers on approval for the surgery. She asked me about it when I was doing rounds. She was very apologetic about bringing it up when I asked her if anything was bothering her at the moment—hesitant about asking me about a personal matter—but she was very frustrated and upset and that kind of thing can preoccupy you. So I took a brief moment out of my day to make sure someone helped her and got her an answer. She was very grateful, and this issue that was consuming her was resolved. Do they always work out that way? Of course not. But it was a case when an employee needed help, and my job as a servant leader was to help her. Do I think that made a difference in her performance going forward? Absolutely. When an organization shows it cares about her—shows that they are more than a faceless number—it can mean everything.

One other thing about being an executive who stays in your bubble. You will breed distrust among workers. Suspicion loves a vacuum, and your isolation will lead to odd theories and rumors about you and the leadership of your organization. Leading from your desk just is not really leading.

As I mentioned, at a hospital where I served as CEO, I had two doors—one to the C-Suite and one to the hallway, which passed by on the way to the cafeteria. I left both open if I was not in a meeting or on an important phone call. People would poke their heads in the door to say hello on their way to lunch or to bring up something at work or to just share a joke. Everybody called me "Dave." It was widely known that I was an Ohio State football fan, and I would get grief about that in the fall during the season. Those types of things make you a real human being. Then, when you have to have difficult conversations, an important connection is there to help those conversations be productive. If you have to ask them to make sacrifices or their job gets tougher, you are much more apt to get cooperation and support because they know you are with them, and you are not asking without consideration for them.

And don't forget that communicating is fun . . .

For those wary of these conversations, I cannot emphasize enough that they are a net positive. I very rarely had anyone rant and rave to me. The conversations were respectful, productive, and often enjoyable. They involved everyone from maintenance guys to doctors. It was everybody, and it helped prevent me from having a narrow view of the operation I led. I understood its intricacies better, and that made me a better leader and decision-maker. I did not know anything about maintenance, but I learned by speaking with people in that department. I did not just learn that they had to fix something. I learned that something had needed to be repaired. I could ask why it needed to be fixed, what caused the problems, and I could learn something new from that conversation about the way our hospital worked.

My conversations with employees motivated me as much or more than anything else I did at work. I am convinced that to be successful as a leader, you have to like people—and I really like people. Speaking with them and listening to their honest feedback and thoughts motivate me. I like hearing from them and knowing more about who they are. I like to get their perspective because it broadens mine. I understand who they are and what they go through.

The forum can vary—one-on-one, small groups, departmental meetings, town halls—but if you are truly connecting with them then you will feel as invigorated by the experience as I do. I used to hold town halls three or four times a year with multiple sessions each time. I would do up to ten of them in a two-week period, and it would wear me out. But the employees expected it, and they showed up. They asked questions and shared their experiences. Sometimes, we laughed. I was physically exhausted by the end of that stretch, but I also was excited and focused on the work ahead—with new ideas and renewed commitment for our mission and organization.

"Talking" points to remember

Great communication is necessary to the success of any organization and its culture because it will improve employee morale and productivity by ensuring simply "they know what it is going on." As this chapter discussed, there are many ways to communicate, both to individuals and as a group. It is critical that as many tactics as possible be utilized because there is not a single best way for optimal communication to occur.

The ultimate guidelines for a loving and compassionate leader to follow are to provide timely, transparent, honest, and vulnerable communication. As David Buzzelli, a former board member, said after I retired from McLaren Northern Michigan hospital, "I particularly liked your openness with the board. You were not hesitant to share your concerns and ask for advice. That does not happen with most CEOs." I hope you now have a better understanding as to the importance of both organizational communication and personal communication as a major contributor to the success of any organization.

Key points to remember when developing your communication tactics:

1. A lack of specific and targeted recognition communication shows employees their performance is not important.
2. Leaders must overcome a fear of being vulnerable for honest communication to be effective.

Proven methods to communicate effectively:

1. Hold regular town hall meetings.
2. Provide regular email communication via daily personal emails.
3. Send handwritten notes to employees recognizing their work.
4. Maintain a high level of visibility through open door policies, formal and informal walking around, and personally addressing everyone you encounter through the 10 and 5 Rule.
5. Get to know your employees other than just through work items—it shows you genuinely care.

CHAPTER SIX

SERVANT LEADERSHIP

CAN YOU BE A LOVING and compassionate leader without being a servant leader? The answer is a resounding no. A recent Google study found that the top attributes of "best leaders" in order of importance were:

- ◆ Servant leadership: facilitating the success of those you lead.
- ◆ Listening well and allowing colleagues to make accurate and relevant decisions.
- ◆ Technical knowledge.

As you can see, while possessing a high level of technical knowledge related to the work that a leader's team does is important, a devotion to servant leadership will ultimately lead to higher productivity and better organizational results.

Bobbie Shreiner, CEO of Progressive Partners, said, "Servant leadership means that everyone you are leading is your boss." This means that your number one priority as a servant leader is the success of those you lead. This can be accomplished by doing things like spending time finding ways that you can support your team rather than spending time defining their expectations. It means asking for feedback to solve a problem rather than simply telling your team what to do. In fact, a willingness to listen to what your team needs rather than singlehandedly deciding what you think they need is the most important start to being a successful servant leader.

A leader must be humble enough to know that he or she is not always right. There are some leaders who think they are always right, because of the position they have. They think it either grants them some magical wisdom or they believe they ascended to the position because of an inability to be wrong. But we are all human beings. We all make mistakes. And the mark of a very smart human being is to recognize their weaknesses and their faults and to admit that they have made mistakes—and then be determined to correct them.

Showing humility through listening

Dr. Scott Nygaard, chief operating officer for Lee Health in Fort Myers, Florida, said that as part of his commitment to servant leadership, he employs a process called "listening tours." This process takes time, which is always a challenge for leaders, but Dr. Nygaard believes that taking the time to listen is an act of service to others: "The reality is it must be true authentic listening, non-defensive and just hearing what is on people's mind—the good (going well), the bad (could improve), and the ugly (needs to stop and/or be changed). Listening is hard, but a strong signal can be sent to the organization by servant leaders with a message that says: "'I care about you and what you think.'" Following up on issues even if the answer is no is critical and shows your listening is sincere. That builds invaluable trust.

Pamela Ream, former director of rehabilitation services at Ozarks Medical Center in West Plains, Missouri, shared a personal story of servant leadership through listening. She met with her team to discuss a very important documentation change that needed to occur in her team's daily work.

Ms. Ream started the meeting by saying "Here is what I think we should do." Immediately, one of her team members said, "Why did you tell us instead of asking?" At that point, Ms. Ream realized that she was not listening to her team and promptly asked for suggestions regarding the best way to make the change that would be most helpful and effective for the team members. All attendees, including Ms. Ream, agreed on a collaborative solution. Do you think this would have happened if Ms. Ream did not support being a servant leader?

I served as CEO at a hospital where we had two orthopedic surgeons whose clinical outcomes were under question by primary care physicians. In general, the primary care physicians were not satisfied with the outcomes that their patients were seeing from these surgeons. They essentially wanted to remove these surgeons from the medical staff. That is a hard thing to do. There are legal intricacies that make it a complex process. In addition, these surgeons generated a huge amount of revenue, and we were entering a brand-new building project. This put me in a tight spot, and that was the immediate perspective that I brought to the conversation. We had some long, intense discussions about it in the physician-CEO cabinet meetings that I hosted.

From that discussion—and from listening to the physicians with an open mind—it became clear to all of us that the right decision was to let the surgeons go. From a clinical perspective and for the benefit of the hospital and the community, it was the right thing to do. The thing that I remember about that meeting so clearly is that the quality of the conversation got us to the point where that decision was clear—where we had a true consensus, despite the varying opinions that we had brought to the room. I always will remain very grateful for conversations like those. Those meetings showed that when you have trust and a willingness to commit to honest, open conversations about difficult topics then you can come to the right decision together, rather than simply staking out your sides of a debate and arguing into eternity.

That must start with a servant leader's sense of humility. If you have that, active listening is second nature. I cannot emphasize enough that the number one way to ensure that people distrust you is to fail to listen to them with any sort of intent. Do not think for a second that you can listen without paying attention and get away with it. People recognize immediately when you are being genuine. They will always see right through someone who is not actually interested in their words and thoughts.

Ditto with a leader who comes into a meeting with a decision already made.

If you want to enrage the people you lead, pretend to come to them for their input on a decision and then go with the decision you had already made in your mind. I will admit that I have gone into meetings with a closed mind in this way. I already had thought through the topic at hand, rolled through the options in my head and considered the various possibilities, and I arrived with my mind made up. That breeds distrust, dishonesty, and disrespect in your team. It may work once, but it will never work in the long term. I am not saying your decision might not be the right one. However, if you are going to put a matter in front of others for discussion and consideration, then you need to commit earnestly to that discussion and weigh the alternatives rather than simply treat them as nuisances that need to be deflected away.

Your team can tell the difference, and they will understand if your decision differs with their advice as a result of an honest, trusting discussion. More likely, though, the best decision is going to incorporate not only your ideas but theirs. Often, the solution will incorporate ideas from throughout the room. You may take good parts of three or four different ideas and combine them into the ideal one. The key is that the best idea wins, no matter whose idea it is. You have to be humble enough to recognize that you do not have all of the answers and you are not always right.

Part of what makes it absolutely critical to listen to each of the options and ideas that come from your team in these meetings is they have spent time and energy to work on the challenges at hand and that effort should always be rewarded. They prepared for the meeting, so respect what they have to say. Remind yourself that any leadership position is a gift and a privilege. Not everyone can be a good one, and we need good leaders desperately in our world today. And people want good leadership. Be proud that they are looking to you to provide it and treat that with the honor and care it deserves.

The requirements of effective servant leadership

Effective servant leadership requires leaders to do the following:

◆ Always think of those you lead first before yourself.
◆ Remind yourself that any leadership position is a gift and a privilege.
◆ Reject chasing material possessions ahead of resources that your team needs to be successful.
◆ Do not care about accolades for yourself but do provide accolades to those you serve first.
◆ Ensure that members of the organization have the tools and resources to be successful.

I will expand on each of these:

Always think of those you lead first before yourself. Investopedia defines servant leadership as someone who "intends to promote the well-being of those around him or her. Servant leadership involves the leader demonstrating the characteristics of empathy, listening, stewardship, and commitment to personal growth toward others." I once received a note from a leader who had attended a Leadership Development Institute (LDI), a quarterly one-day leadership development program at the hospital where I served as the president and CEO, that read, "Thank you for speaking at our LDI and being our leader! Your support of our leadership team to be the very best they can be is evident by the enthusiasm and passion you bring to sessions."

Sometimes all it takes to be an effective servant leader is to provide genuine, consistent, and enthusiastic support for those you lead. A leadership program often requires a significant investment of time and resources, which is a true labor of love. A servant leader is willing to sacrifice time and their own personal resources to support the development and success of those they lead. Those kinds of gestures and efforts can go a long way.

Reject chasing material possessions. Chasing money can be a temptation for any leader. Leaders' compensation often is based on a host of incentives and that can lead to them chasing the results that trigger those incentives rather than the resources that your team actually needs to be successful. One that always drove me crazy is that I often was under pressure to generate a budgeted operating margin, and it was difficult sometimes to keep that from overshadowing other considerations in decisions. It was tough to keep my focus from tightening too much on that looming metric.

I will give you an example. There was a clinical service called endocrinology that was extremely expensive because of the general shortage of endocrinologists. They received a high salary because there was such high demand for them in the healthcare community, especially from primary care physicians. They also perform an essential service: treating people with diabetes and insulin issues. However, they do not generate a lot of revenue. Their work largely revolves around office visits and testing, not the most lucrative revenue components of a hospital's budget. Ultimately, the practice was costing the hospital a significant amount of money.

I found myself wondering about the wisdom of keeping the endocrinology practice onboard because of the cost to our operation. That operating margin was where my eyes went. However, my gaze did not stay there. I was convinced by some passionate physicians and staff of the incredible service to the community that the practice served and of the crucial part it played in our overall healthcare system. Without it, they would not have anywhere to refer their patients with diabetes. They made it clear that keeping and supporting the practice was simply the right thing to do, no matter what its impact on the operating margin and the executive team's incentives. That practice was representative of why we were in business in the first place.

I resisted simply because I fell into the money trap. However, ultimately, I was talked into a model that worked. We decided that we would be willing to absorb some financial losses because we listened to our primary care physicians and the concerns from our patients in the community and recognized that we should not eliminate a program that served the chronic care needs of the community.

Do not care about accolades for yourself but do provide accolades to those you serve first. This is an easy thing to do, unless you have insecurities that provide roadblocks. I loved being able to publicly recognize with accolades the people that I served, and I was never comfortable receiving any accolades before my team did. Part of this was recognizing that any accolades for me really belonged to the entire team. It was important for me that they were recognized first because they did the work, and I wanted to make sure they knew they were appreciated.

Being the leader of a successful team should be all that you need. The way I saw it is that I just tried to provide the leadership, but they really did the hard work.

Some leaders care more about accolades for themselves because they are always looking to "move up." Their current position is just the latest steppingstone to bigger and better positions. Their decisions are all driven by that short-term goal of strengthening their resumé and their bona fides to capture new accolades and use them to leap to something new and more prominent. That might work for them in the short term, but in the long term, it is an attitude that will come back to bite them. Their reputation for having a self-serving, self-centered attitude will grow and attach to them, following them everywhere they go.

Failing to recognize those you serve for the work that they do is a reliable way to torpedo your career.

Ensure that all members of the organization have the tools and resources to be successful. They will appreciate this more than you can ever imagine, and it also is an absolute, nonnegotiable requirement of a servant leader. Your job is to help them do their jobs to the best of their abilities, and they cannot do that if you do not provide the necessary support. It can be too easy to lose sight of that. That means open, steady conversation to make sure you know what they need and do not fall out of touch. Their needs are always changing, and that means you have to be consistently aware of those changing needs. You have to ask them questions and seek them out, not just passively expect the answers to come to you. Sometimes, they may not realize where they are missing the tools and resources you need. You can help them identify those needs with your involvement and attention.

It may seem like common sense, but too often leaders forget that they will not be successful if their teams are not successful. It is the definition of a win-win for everyone.

Choosing unselfishness

Scott MacLellan, CEO for Touchpoint Support Services & Morrison Living for the Compass Group, follows the servant leadership model by believing his role is to help others grow and by demonstrating a willingness to have tough conversations to ensure alignment with company culture and values. This means to appreciate each person's unique gifts and provide ample opportunities for people to let their light shine. MacLellan said that a servant leader provides support for growth in areas where associates and leaders need or want to improve. He advises not to give someone a task that you know they are not prepared for or have the ability to do. Instead, always provide the tools or resources necessary for their best chance of success and then celebrate that success with them.

Those of you reading this chapter probably think that being a servant leader sounds great and the right thing to do. It is! However, it is challenging for a leader who is driven by personal results that lead to either financial benefit or career growth. It is easy for someone who is so focused on the "next step up" to lose their moral compass toward serving others. In reality, some of us have acted this way, especially those like me who were looking for that "next big promotion." I once left a job to accept what I believed was a better career opportunity but left my wonderful team in a difficult spot to complete some very important work. It was not my proudest moment as a servant leader because I left them in a vulnerable position so I could fulfill my own selfish career goals.

Someone who believes they want to be a servant leader has to first "choose to be unselfish" per Joel Manby. It is difficult to be this type of leader if one is not unselfish in their personal lives, such as through a commitment to volunteering or philanthropy. There are so many opportunities to be a servant leader outside of your profession that allow you to make a significant and positive impact on someone's life and to make the world a better place. The biggest challenge to being a servant leader outside of work is the enormity of those who need help. To this point, Andy Stanley, senior pastor of North Point Community Church in Alpharetta, Georgia, offered advice. He said, "Do for one what you wish you could do for everyone."

I am going to share two quick personal stories of servant leadership to show how little things can go a long way in the minds of those you lead. First, I always told the members of our hospital foundation, the major philanthropy arm of our hospital, that I "work for you." In other words, when a potential donor wanted to talk with me as the CEO, I would work fully around the schedule of that donor and the foundation staff member who was working with that donor, sometimes even meeting the same day. Why is this important? First, it could help the hospital financially, and it helps support the success for the foundation staff person, which is a win-win. As an aside, my servant leadership helped support a very successful new hospital building capital campaign, which achieved its fundraising goal in 2019.

The second example is more operational. The purchasing director for the operating rooms was getting "beat up" by the orthopedic surgeons for not having the correct type and number of supplies for shoulder surgeries. The surgeons had a legitimate complaint because the problem was delaying surgeries for patients who needed this surgery within a reasonable period of time. The purchasing director informed me of the problem and said that he was not getting satisfactory answers from corporate purchasing. I contacted the corporate director of purchasing who found that there were issues he was not fully aware of in the ordering process, which he promptly resolved. The operating room purchasing director sent me a note saying "Thanks for your support on these issues. I have worked here for six years and have never received this level of support from administration and the CEO . . . it is a great breath of fresh air."

I did not share this example for my own glorification, but to show how servant leadership supporting the needs of those doing the work is so important to that person's success and ultimately, the organization's success. As a leader, you often are in a unique position to help people succeed. Embrace that opportunity.

Servant leaders are successful leaders

Along with being personally gratifying, a servant leader has a greater chance of personal success. It stands to reason that when the leaders you lead are successful, then the organization and you will be successful. Someone you provide servant leadership to is promoted—do you think you will benefit financially and professionally because of this person's success? Of course you will. From a leadership perspective, there is no greater joy than seeing someone you serve grow in their career to greater heights for themselves and the organization. Frankly, being a servant leader is a "no brainer" for success—for the organization, the leader you serve, and you.

I have discussed it before, but servant leaders must recognize when they are allowing their personal ambition to get in the way of the success of the organization. The cliché is that it is "lonely at the top." In reality, it is lonely at the top if you make it lonely. It is very easy to become isolated and selfish when you have a senior leadership position with major, consequential responsibilities. There is no question about that. Again, though, it is totally avoidable. If you are a servant leader, and you strive to see the organization through the eyes of those you lead, you will never feel alone. That takes effort, though. That means getting out and poking your head in doors and stopping people in the hallways and picking up the phone and making calls. That means talking to everyone from the members of your C-suite to workers in much less glamorous positions. That means asking them questions, getting their opinions, keeping your ear to the ground, and forever searching for better ways of doing things through conversations rather than sitting at your desk and wracking your own limited brain.

We all should be able to recognize at this point that servant leadership and personal ambition are not mutually exclusive. You do not at all have to sacrifice your goals in order to be a servant leader. Servant leaders are successful leaders, and arrogant leaders who do not care about the people who support them are unsuccessful ones. That is true for every level of leadership—from CEOs to unit supervisors. If you are interested in your own success and climbing the management ranks, then your focus must be on your team—not yourself.

My first management job was serving as the night shift supervisor in a respiratory therapy department at a community hospital in Cleveland. I had six therapists to cover the service 24/7. I depended on them to be successful. The department only did its job—and I only performed mine—if those therapists did. So that was my focus—serving them.

The ultimate of servant leadership was Jesus Christ. On the night before he was crucified and died, he washed the feet of his disciples. Jesus said, "Instead, whoever wants to be great among you must be your servant, and whoever wants to be first must be slave of all" (Mark 9:35 New International Version).

Servant leadership is a calling to support the greatness of those one serves, which benefits our world all the way down to the organizations we support in our professional life.

CHAPTER SEVEN

WALK THE TALK

A PERSON WHO DESIRES TO be a loving and compassionate leader must consistently set the standard by "walking the talk." What exactly does "walking the talk" mean? Simply put, it means that this type of leader lives and breathes love and compassion in their daily work—with "daily" being a key component. This sounds easier than it is because interactions with those one leads sometimes are difficult and emotional situations.

Walking the talk involves visible actions that require commitment and focus. Let's face it, leaders are always on stage as to how they are being perceived as a leader. This means that it takes a tremendous amount of constant dedication to this leadership value, whether it is in front of one person or a thousand. This means there is no special sauce for walking the talk other than just doing it! Subsequently, this chapter will mostly be focused on real-life examples of leaders who walk the talk—with a few not-so-positive examples included.

The dangers of "Do as I say, not as I do"

There are too many leaders both in healthcare and outside of it who adhere to the "Do as I say, not as I do" philosophy. We all see it every day. It is, of course, unrealistic to expect that the people you lead will perform at their best and have the highest job engagement if they see that you are not doing the things that you are asking them to do—if you are not meeting the very standards that you have established for them to meet.

I think it is important that all leaders follow the simple rule that you do not ask someone to do something that you would not be willing to do. I do not mean specific specialized tasks, such as perform surgery, but I do mean behaviors, such as showing up to work on time, listening respectfully to colleagues, or dressing professionally. I am not a nurse nor am I a doctor or a house-keeper. However, I can model leadership for people in each of those positions and set an example of how we can all do the best jobs that we can do while treating people with respect, compassion, and kindness.

I think people—and we are seeing this more in our society today—people resent somebody who says, "Do as I say, not as I do." That can be dangerous in a workplace, particularly in one that can feature challenging conditions. If you have strict policies in place that employees must arrive in their job areas by 8:00 a.m.—perhaps with penalties for tardiness—but everyone sees you "strolling" in at 9:00 a.m., regardless of whether you worked until ten the night before, then you are going to have problems. As a leader, you need to be sensitive to that and to the careful way you are watched to model behavior for others. Your commitment will prove closely linked to their commitment.

Active compassion

To start, I believe that the most important attribute for a leader who walks the talk is to exhibit active encouragement and enthusiasm. This must be genuine. How many of you or those you serve feel that they have had "too much encouragement" in their lives, especially lately? The answer, of course, is not many. Because of the privileged position one has as a leader, we have a wonderful opportunity to make someone's life better. Making someone's life better is contagious, increases energy for the giver and receiver, and will lead to greater job effectiveness and productivity. The way you do it is to acknowledge and get to know every single colleague or employee that you encounter. This can easily be done with just a smile, a simple hello, or a short conversation.

Gene Kaminski, retired vice president of human resources for McLaren Northern Michigan hospital, said, "Compassion for others is an action activity that includes empathy and understanding to someone's condition, past, current, or future. This will not work unless they get to personally know employees." According to Scott MacLellan, CEO for Touchpoint Support Services & Morrison Living for the Compass Group, "A leader must get to know beyond a superficial level your associates and leaders in order to build strong relationships. The word 'encouragement' itself can be defined as an obligation or agreement. I have found that the engagement of my team has increased in proportion to my own commitment to improve myself and fulfill my obligation to love, protect, encourage, grow, serve, and appreciate them."

You see that walking the talk sounds so straightforward, but it is challenging for some leaders who are focused more on results than people.

Focus on personal growth

I think every committed leader should be a continual learner—always learning about the pulse of your team and the organization that you lead. I have heard about a CEO of a large healthcare system who has been in his role for several years, and nobody knows him. It is an ongoing discussion in certain circles. They call him the man behind the curtain. I do not know how that organization can be successful without an executive team that makes up for his lack of engagement. Continuous learning about what is happening in your organization is everything for an executive. What are the challenges your team members are facing? What resources do they need? How can I get better at supporting them and our mission?

Personal growth also is essential. Too many people are reluctant to allow themselves to learn—to be taught. You should forever be reading books and searching out other material that help you better understand how to be a better leader and person. You should forever seek out new sources of motivation and inspiration. Motivational leadership articles, for instance, were very important to me personally. They helped keep me focused and driven to fulfill my obligation to love, protect, serve, and appreciate my work and the people I led.

Personal growth is necessary to remain fully engaged and committed to your work—you cannot have one without the other. Otherwise, your effort will fall short, and you will settle into a rut of completing tasks and managing the day-to-day without larger, more meaningful goals.

Walking the talk when the pressure is on

Commitment to walking the talk can also waver when the pressure and attention is turned up. It is easy to walk the talk at an inconsequential meeting on a Friday afternoon, but it is much more difficult when you are in a crisis with no visible end in sight. People have a tendency then to retreat from their principles and process. They move away from their mantra of walking the talk. They lose their patience, they become quick to anger, and they sacrifice their trustfulness of other people. They stop listening the same way, burrowing deeper into their own thoughts and concerns.

No question about it, it is hard to walk the talk when you are staring a crisis in the face. However, walking the talk becomes even more important in the times of the greatest stress and tension. You need to model good behavior for your team more than ever because that is how you are going to navigate the crisis together. The tough times are when your team will most look to you for leadership, so it is vitally important that you provide it.

The COVID-19 pandemic has proven to demonstrate some amazing examples of leadership in the healthcare world. The pandemic caused hospitals to face enormous challenges—likely some of the great challenges in their existences. And most have absolutely risen to the occasion in stunning fashion. The leadership of those hospitals has played an essential part in that success. I know many CEOs who have made a point of putting in as many long hours as the nurses and doctors and other care providers in their hospitals. They work in command centers, laboring with their teams to manage an endless array of challenges and difficult decisions. They are deeply involved in the treatment, testing, and vaccination processes, and they are giving it everything they have to make sure that our frontline heroes have all of the resources that they need to do their jobs. Walking the talk in a time of a crisis is so, so critical.

Failing to follow through on your mission

The first example of an organization not following the walk-the-talk value on the macro level involves a faith-based hospital system. The system is proud of their mission to serve and provide healthcare for the poor—but only *if* the operating margin is above 3 percent. Yes, we all know about the "no margin, no mission" mantra, but not providing for the poor when there is a margin of 3 percent or less appears to not follow their mission, especially when the system is a not-for-profit. This creates "tension" between following the mission and focusing on margin.

I am a big believer in faith-based healthcare. I think faith helps heal the sick. Now that being said, you still have to generate a reasonable margin to operate and fulfill your mission. There is obvious tension that comes because of that. How large of a margin do you need to be successful and keep the doors open? How large of a margin do you need to ensure that you are not just providing care but excellent care? That everybody on your team has what they need to provide that excellent care? If you need a certain margin, does that mean you must sacrifice compassion along the way?

It is a clear, ongoing dilemma when you are in a faith-based healthcare organization, or even any type of not-for-profit community hospital. Your hospital's mission is to clearly serve the healthcare needs of the community. It is your reason for existing. When you focus on that message and you continuously reiterate that to your organization, and then you go into the boardroom or the executive meeting and you are cutting programs because they do not make money, regardless of their importance to the community and the people you serve, then that is an obvious problem. You are not walking the talk as an organization or as a leader. You lose the trust of those you lead, and you also muddy the waters of their work—of the purpose and reason for their jobs. It is a reminder that you cannot say one thing and do another and lead an organization with any effectiveness.

I faced this type of dilemma many times in my career. One example was when I was leading a hospital network that included a small community hospital with a labor and delivery program that did not birth many babies. Consequently, it achieved poor financial results. Subsequently, we eliminated the birthing program. The community response went through the roof. The thing about birthing programs is that they generally do not make much money—you get paid poorly—but it is a crucial investment in the community. It is one of those programs that when you are a community hospital you often are "the only game in town." It is essential for people. So even though this hospital was not seeing a lot of activity, the activity that it was seeing meant a lot to the community. Without it, expectant mothers and their families would have to travel much farther for their service. That was a hard decision—and to this day I wonder if it was the right one or if we made a mistake.

Approachability and accessibility

The final point to make is that important principles of being a walk the talk leader are approachability and accessibility. Philip Incarnati, president and CEO of McLaren Health Care, said that approachability and accessibility are the two values that show you genuinely care about how employees see you. Sometimes, just knowing that you are available to hear their concerns or thoughts is enough to show them you care as part of your walking the talk behavior. The sad thing is many leaders say they have "an open door" policy but do not follow it because of either time constraints or just a reluctance or fear to talk with someone who may be unhappy and/or upset. Believe me, it is a human resource negative and de-motivator when the boss hides in the office.

Dave Frescoln, retired business executive and former board chairman of McLaren Northern Michigan hospital, shared that he was once made aware of a new department director that during his first meeting, held up his paycheck and said, "I make more than you which makes me better than you and I am the king." So . . . other than the obvious arrogance of this new director, do you think he was encouraging his team and walking the talk? It is hard to imagine a leader—or anyone—being so disrespectful and expecting to receive respect in return. Who wants to work for a leader like that? Who would be remotely motivated to put in a good, honest effort to support a leader so unimaginably selfish? I do not know how successful this person ended up being, but I have a hard time believing his career as a leader was a long, thriving one.

One day approximately ten years ago, my wife Rhonda was walking with me inside a hospital I served as the CEO. She noticed that I said hello and acknowledged everyone I encountered and that they would acknowledge me back by my first name. These were normal interactions for me, but Rhonda was taken aback. I asked her why. She said that in a hospital where she once worked, the CEO never acknowledged colleagues in the hallway. In fact, she would not have even recognized the CEO in order to greet him. Rhonda also observed meaningful encouragement and leader engagement because the employees would call me by my first name. Walking the talk involves taking time, no matter how small or large, to acknowledge and get to know the members of the team you serve.

Employees recognizing their CEO and connecting with them in the hallway is much more than a small, nice thing. It is more meaningful than that. It is more meaningful than I think anybody realizes. I believe that we persistently underestimate the power of this kind of connection. It has positive ramifications that spread—the ripples in the pond metaphor. It shows the kind of engagement that naturally boosts productivity. If someone is comfortable enough to say hello to their CEO in the hallway and to call them by their first name, then they are comfortable enough to have meaningful conversations with them. They are comfortable enough to share their opinions and vital information that can help the CEO do their job better. It also shows that the employee feels supported and cared for in their jobs. It shows that they believe their work is valued. If you strictly are an office-dweller who engages in formal, programmed conversations throughout the day, then you are not walking the talk.

The good news is that I have many terrific examples of how walking the talk as a servant leader makes a difference. Remember, the key is to always be genuine. Kim Thompson, former chief financial officer at Ozarks Medical Center in West Plains, Missouri, said that her CEO was a "loving and compassionate person that made leadership effortless. This CEO was genuine because he knew as many names as possible, and more importantly, he looked those he served in the eye with the truth." Thompson and William Geschke also shared that part of walking the talk was again getting to know people on a personal level that includes work, learning, play, sports, hobbies, interests, and family interactions, such as picnics and gatherings, because it helps to humanize people, especially leaders.

Other examples from my work as a CEO include the following feedback: "Never had a president and CEO of a hospital been so personable and caring." "Your speaking style gives people the feeling you are having a conversation with them rather than a lecture." "Thank you for making a difference with your positive and caring attitude." "Thank you for taking time out of your busy day to talk to a patient who is a fellow Ohio State Buckeye fan—you really outdid yourself on this one!" "I just wanted to thank you for being such a hands-on leader. Your time, energies, and even your funny jokes are all appreciated." "Thanks for your leadership. You set a great example of how to be a great leader."

My final example is one that I am probably most proud of. It was sent to me by a staff nurse after I helped her with the transport of a patient: "I know this was probably just you being you, but I wanted to say 'thank you' again for your assistance this evening helping transport our patient into his room today after surgery! What an awesome way to meet you! I was very impressed and grateful to see you going out of your way in a suit and jumping right into bedside care for your top clients . . . our patients! In my eight years of service here, I have to say I have never seen this happen, not that it hasn't, but wow, what a way to implement our standards of patient care. Sorry to say, but we will be bragging about this up here on 2North. Thank you from our staff and most importantly, our patient!"

Now my reason for sharing the different positive comments from my CEO tenure was not to glorify me but to show how much of a difference you can make with those you serve, both employees and clients, by just walking the talk. You are always noticed, both for the great things you do and the not-so-great things you do. Additionally, I feel compelled and happy to share that there were times when employees reminded me that I was not walking the talk, which I very much appreciated. What comes to mind is that there were times when I would be walking down the hallway deep in thought with my eyes down, which violated our 10 and 5 Rule of people acknowledgment. When this happened, an employee would say "Hi Dave, eyes up!" My point is that we are human, and that walking the talk 100 percent of the time may not be totally realistic, but we should all do our best to meet that standard to ensure the best chance of success for the organization. Plus, it is always the right thing to do as a leader to treat people with dignity and kindness.

Walk the talk takeaways

John V. Bednar, a retired school principal in Cleveland, Ohio, outlined his "walk the talk" values, which I believe are excellent to consider as you go forward on your own walk the talk journey:

1. Always be on time. Being late shows a lack of concern for the other meeting attendees' time.

2. Dress for success. Can you remember a leader who did not dress professionally? There is a belief or perception that someone who dresses sloppily or inappropriately will manage their work the same way. True or not, a leader does not want their employees to feel that way because it may have a trickle-down effect throughout the company.

3. Ask for help. Asking for help shows you are not perfect and are humble enough to request it before disaster occurs.

4. Build a professional network. This shows how vested you are in your own professional growth when you can call on your network for advice and counsel.

5. Be willing to forgive. Can you forgive when someone you trusted caused you embarrassment or failure? This is part of moving forward both in business and life.

6. Share talents. Share and utilize every member of your team's talents and ideas. The person sharing will gain confidence knowing their talent helped support the success of others.

7. Be confident. Being confident does not mean being arrogant or a "know it all." Those you lead want to follow a confident leader but also someone who is humble and understands his or her weaknesses.

8. Keep promises or do not make them. It is acceptable not to keep a promise as long as you communicate the "why." Not following through with a promise lowers a leader's credibility almost immediately. It can be difficult to overcome a broken promise.

9. Control your anger and emotions. This is one of the hardest to follow for me. I am a very passionate and driven leader. However, there were occasions when I let my anger for an outcome I did not like or want be visible. This does very little to support the confidence of your team in you or to support finding a reasonable solution to the problem.

10. Lose like a winner and take accountability for that loss. A servant leader and a leader who walks the talk never takes all of the credit for a winning solution because it takes a team to achieve that result. Likewise, it is never a good thing to not take accountability for a mistake or

loss. Blaming others shows you are self-centered and not confident in yourself or your team.

11. Change a bad habit. Bad habits turn into bad actions. A most obvious example occurred in the recent pandemic of 2020. Leaders were requiring employees and citizens to wear masks, yet many of them were unwilling to support the habit of wearing a mask by wearing one themselves. So . . . does this send a message that everyone else must comply but not you?

12. Say lots of good mornings and thank yous. Many times, the morning or afternoon greeting and show of appreciation will make someone's day in a positive way and make you feel better as well.

13. Be the number one cheerleader for your organization. How can an organization even think about being successful when the leader is not actively and visibly supporting the organization? We all know of a leader in our past who is miserable and who openly remarks that they are counting down the days to retirement. How do you think the employees feel who have ten, twenty, or even thirty years more to work?

A loving and compassionate leader cannot expect those that follow to achieve their maximum potential unless that leader consistently and genuinely walks the talk during both wonderful and profitable times and difficult and unprofitable times. The team will know how to follow if you are walking the talk as a loving and compassionate leader.

CHAPTER EIGHT

COMMITMENT

BY NOW I HOPE THAT you are excited and inspired about being a loving and compassionate leader based on what you read and learned in the first seven chapters of this book. The real challenge is staying committed during the times you are tempted to revert back to your previous leadership style when the "going gets tough" again. In order to be successful with your new leadership style, both to yourself and to those you lead, you must stay dedicated to your values no matter what the circumstance. This is sometimes easier said than done.

True commitment is to act consistently in alignment with the same set of values at work, in the community, and in your personal life. In many cases, this value overlaps with the "walking the talk" value, but the commitment value shows that you are "all in" to being a loving and compassionate leader. It also shows the colleagues you lead that you will not sway from these values no matter what the circumstances.

Being committed is at the core of leadership. If you are not committed to being the best leader that you can be, then you are not committed to the organization. You are not committed to the people you serve, and you will not get results. My belief is that if you are not committed to the mission and vision of an organization and to the people you serve in the organization, then you should not be there at all. You cannot be half in as a leader. You have to be all the way in. Otherwise, it just does not work.

Leaders lacking commitment

Is being committed easy? In most cases, I would argue that it is not. Let us take a look at some poor examples of commitment. As this book is being written, the United States and the world is gripped in the throes of a pandemic. It is a very difficult, challenging, un-precedented, and uncertain time in our country and the world. It has been exacerbated because it is an election year in the United States which has led to the pandemic being politicized in many instances. This has led to inconsistent leadership decision-making between political leaders, public health professionals, and the people who believe their freedoms as an individual as written in the Constitution are being threatened.

The increase in COVID-19 infections was spiking significantly as the 2020 Thanksgiving holiday approached. Many of our elected leaders strongly suggested and even mandated in some cases not to have large family Thanksgiving gatherings, which including discouraging family members to not travel by land or air to visit family. Subsequently, the following are examples of leaders who did not walk the talk and ultimately "decommitted" to their public and personal leadership mandates.

One of these leaders was a governor who was spotted having dinner in public in a closed room with about ten other people in a restaurant, with none of them wearing a mask. This came after telling the citizens in his state to wear a mask and only take it off when chewing their food and to not to dine in indoor restaurants. Even worse, the governor was accompanied by public health officials and physicians. Another example was a mayor of a large city that mandated small Thanksgiving gatherings and no travel. Yet, this same person was seen getting on a plane for a Thanksgiving trip to visit his mother. He justified his noncommitment by saying he had not seen his mother in many months. Another governor was seen having dinner in a restaurant with his family. None of them was wearing a face mask even though the governor required it of the state's citizens. When confronted, he did not see this as an issue and was upset that he was confronted by angry patrons in the restaurant who reminded the governor about his closing of bars, restaurants, and gyms. Finally, another mayor went to see his parents at Thanksgiving despite telling everyone else to stay home. He said it was a private and not a public matter. Looks like the mayor's commitment to leadership is only applicable when it benefits him and not those he leads.

Probably the worst example came when a leader in Congress was seen "sneaking" in the back door of a hair salon in a city that shut down all hair salons because of COVID-19, and of course, this famous elected official was not wearing a mask. I share these examples not to be political, but to point out the hypocrisy of the commitment of these leaders to their self-prescribed mandates. "Do as I say and not as I do" creates huge credibility issues for those leaders and ultimately social unrest and societal chaos because of their selfish leadership styles. Leaders who do not walk the talk and are uncommitted will invariably fail, both for themselves as well as the company or organization they lead.

One final example involved a company committed to a major internal and external service initiative. The project included numerous metrics to hold leadership accountable for improved results. The project failed even though the leadership team from the department director level down achieved meaningful results. The program failed because corporate senior management said they supported the project, but they did not commit to it through their personal leadership actions. Examples included never reviewing project results at senior management meetings along with not following guidelines for standards such as meeting agendas, returning emails, and holding themselves accountable for internal employee satisfaction scores.

This particular initiative was organization-wide, but senior management's failure to walk the talk with it essentially condemned it to failure. If people see that senior management will not commit to something, then they never will. If senior leaders are not going to participate, then no one else will. It is a basic truth that too often is ignored out of distraction and preoccupation. In my opinion, there is not a single initiative that should be rolled out in any organization without the one hundred percent full support and commitment of senior management. And that commitment should be visible and explicit. That commitment will filter down and attract the kind of buy-in that leads to success.

Flavor-of-the-month initiatives

A characteristic of many workplaces is the rise and inevitable fall of "flavor-of-the-month" initiatives. These efforts emerge from some new trend or sudden determination to address a lingering problem or inefficiency. Healthcare is notorious for these, but they really are emblematic of every field. We all know what these initiatives look like. Management rolls this new program out, likely with a decent amount of fanfare and lofty proclamations of the progress that awaits ahead. There is a kickoff meeting and initial follow-ups and plans—and then management does not pursue the initiative or fully hold leaders accountable. The entire team realizes that management will never mention it again, and they can get back to doing things the way they were done before. What is worse is that every new initiative will be treated with the suspicion that it is just the latest management fad. They can pretend to pay attention to it in the early going, knowing that there will be no follow-through or accountability from leadership. Through management's lack of commitment, they have created a culture that greets new ideas and initiatives with a reflexive skepticism. Rather than being ready to embrace new efforts and opportunities, team members roll their eyes when they arrive.

I remember at one of my posts when we created an employee engagement survey. We promoted it and encouraged our workers to sit down and put real thought into filling it out. "We need your input," we said. "This will help to build and support the culture of our organization." We received well above an 80 percent response rate, an extremely strong showing and one that deserved to be paid attention to.

But then we dropped the ball. Senior management looked at the data but did not follow up with leaders at the supervisory level to ensure accountability and to drive progress in the areas they led. We did not require or aid the development of action plans to address areas of need. It is very frustrating for me to think about, because it runs counter to what I believe. We had an opportunity, a big one. That is what that employee participation in the survey represented. They believed that their responses would mean something and contribute to the organization. We let them down, no question about it.

So what was the impact when they saw no follow-through on the survey? No doubt it did not inspire confidence in leadership. No question that the next time we asked them for their feedback they were less enthusiastic to provide it. "What's the point?" some of them must have wondered.

Our lack of response is exactly the kind of mistake that breeds cynicism and doubt in the workplace. Putting in the time and effort to avoid that kind of result would have been well worth it.

How to be engaged

Leaders can signal their disinterest in other, more subtle ways, too. Failing to return emails. Skipping items on meeting agendas that they do not feel like addressing. I firmly believe that if a colleague takes the time to send you an email or text than they deserve the professional courtesy of a response. Ignoring their messages falls short of servant leadership. My rule was to respond within twenty-four hours to all messages, though that could be difficult at times. I will admit that this might not be for everybody. I drove my wife crazy more than once staying up at night answering emails. Still, I earned a reputation for being responsive to my colleagues, and that meant a lot to me. It proved to them that I cared about what they have to say. I cannot understand how you can be a strong leader without responding to the people who reach out to you. I know that if I send a note to someone and they do not respond, then my takeaway is that they do not value what I have to say.

Similarly, failing to follow a set agenda for a meeting can send a message that you do not take planning seriously. Often, items on an agenda are there because they are necessary to team members. These are issues that they believe are important to get on the table for discussion. If you cavalierly steamroll past them, you are sending a clear signal to them about how much you appreciate what they value. Some leaders' thought processes will be, "They told me they wanted to talk about this, but we just do not have the time today. I have got other stuff to talk about."

Occasionally, that can be a legitimate scenario, and in that case, you need to be clear why you are skipping certain agenda items and make clear when you will be available to discuss them. Most people will understand. However, if you are asking your leadership team to set agendas for meetings so that they are productive, and you expect to hold people accountable for the ideas that result from those meetings, then it seems more than reasonable that you respect the outlines of the meetings and hold yourself responsible for respecting the agendas of the meetings. Otherwise, soon enough, your team's approach to bringing issues and ideas to the meeting room table will be, "Why bother? We never get anywhere with them." And they will have a point.

The positive side of that is that when the person who submitted a request or a discussion item feels like their issues are heard and considered, then they will do better, more committed work. They will feel engaged.

A common complaint from physicians is that administrators never respond to their concerns. This could be any profession, but physicians are a prime example of where it occurs and causes keen problems. Physicians will repeatedly go to an administrator with a concern and many times never get a response. It is surprising how often this happens. And the reason it happens is because the administrator does not want to respond to the physician with an answer that the physician does not want to hear. They want to avoid unpleasant conversations because they will have to say no to someone.

Leaders everywhere do this, and the people who work for them know when it is happening—when a topic is being avoided or delayed because a manager is reluctant to face it head on. All it does, of course, is extend the pain for the administrator—they need to rip that band-aid off—and teach workers that the administrators are reluctant to engage with tough issues. They avoid the issue because of the challenging conversation they do not want to have, but the person who is being avoided—in this case, a physician—ends up being only more unhappy because of the frustration of being unable to get an answer. For them, the dawdling administrator has lost all credibility.

Commitment always starts at the top or else chances for success diminish significantly if the organization does not see and feel this commitment. Are these examples of leaders who are consistently in alignment with the same set of values at work, in the community, and in their personal lives—which I have explained is a staple of committed leadership?

The power of hope

How does a leader show commitment? Certainly, by their visible actions or lack thereof as pointed out in the previous examples. But what is the primary role of a committed leader? It is to radiate hope! But how?

By providing clarity and full understanding of vision, mission, and values combined with strong financial results. Furthermore, power without love cannot be one of your loving and compassionate leadership values. Dr. Martin Luther King said that "power without love is reckless and abusive, and love without power is sentimental and anemic." It must be remembered that a philosophy of hope, love, and compassion does not mean a leader is weak and soft. Finally, hope if provided by a fully committed leader who leads by example is an example of "walking the talk."

Now, let us review some examples of committed leadership that were successful. Upon assuming the president and CEO position at McLaren Northern Michigan in late 2013, I learned that the physical facility was in desperate need of renovation and new construction in order to provide better service and care to the northern Michigan community. I also learned that due to financial challenges over the previous ten years the project kept being tabled. I knew the community, physicians, and hospital staff believed in the project and would do everything they could to be supportive. That led me to believe in the project and to be fully committed to gaining hospital and corporate board approval to make it become a reality.

How did I show this commitment? I took every opportunity in a passionate, enthusiastic, and business manner to review the project with as many stakeholders as possible. This included board members, corporate executives, hospital providers, community leaders, and legislators. Over time, all of these stakeholders supported and believed in my commitment to the project.

There were many appropriate challenges to the financial viability of the project, but for more than four years we stayed committed to receiving final approval. I am pleased to report that the new hospital building will open in 2022! The learning point here is that everyone I spoke to, whether it was internally or externally, knew my unwavering commitment for a new hospital.

Scott MacLellan, CEO for Touchpoint Support Services & Morrison Living for the Compass Group, said that his organization celebrates leader commitment every year with a "best" story of the year about people leading with love and compassion. These include leaders who may buy things for their patients, residents, and fellow team members. These are leaders who rallied behind their teammates who got sick or lost homes in natural disasters. Compass brings these leaders together into a very big awards event to share their story. MacLellan said that "people who do not lead with love and are not committed to it are all about self. No stories to tell from them because they quickly fade from our organization." Amen!

Commitment can be big or small, but the significance of it never changes. I once attended a Saturday conference in the middle of summer for cardiac surgery outcomes with one of my cardiovascular surgeons. At the time, I thought it would be important as the CEO to show my support for this surgeon and our program. Later that week, the surgeon sent me a wonderful note thanking me for attending and showing my commitment to the program. It was a "big deal" to him.

As I stated earlier, I believe that faith is an integral part of healing in healthcare. Consequently, I am committed to hospital chaplaincy programs as part of patient healing and employee healing. I asked the chaplains to pray for our leadership team and providers and pray with the leadership team before the monthly meetings. I received many expressions of appreciation for including this devotion for our team.

Curiosity and courage are key to commitment

According to the late Charles Lindstrom, the president and CEO of Saint Luke's Hospital in Kansas City, a leader must be curious, courageous, and most importantly, committed. I believe there is no substitute to being a loving, compassionate, and committed leader.

Curiosity means always searching for the right solution and not just settling for the one that you already know. It means always asking, will this improve the organization and provide resources for our people to be successful?

Meanwhile, you have to have a culture in your organization that allows leaders to be courageous without fear of reprisal. That is really important because if your leaders are afraid to make a mistake, then you will never get the best out of them. You will never get their best ideas. You will never get innovative creative solutions. I tried to be mindful of that in my career.

If someone I led made a mistake that was driven by courage, then I wanted to make sure that they were not punished for it. If it did not work, it did not work. We would go back through why it did not work, explore where an idea failed, and perhaps even seek to modify it and build on it. And I like to think that I made it clear that I welcomed courageous ideas and decision-making because it really is the only way you can progress as an organization. It is where creative, innovative thinking is born.

Some advice on commitment from some wise people

Seek the right solution, take reasonable risks willingly, and use creative imagination, per Sir Winston Churchill: "If there is not wind, row." That means that if you do not have momentum and things are not going your way—if you are just sitting still in the water, no wind at your back—then you need to put in the hard work to find a way forward. If you do not, then you will never get anywhere, because there will be many more times when there is no wind than when a nice, steady breeze is simply carrying you along and making life easy for you. Fortunately, necessity is where innovation comes from. It is the source of innovation and the best ideas. So be grateful for the lack of wind and be excited for the chance to row.

Perceive the blind spots or as Yogi Berra noted: "You can observe a lot just by watching."

Lisa Motley, former executive director, Department of Cardiovascular and Thoracic Surgery, University of Louisville, said that a leader can show commitment by seeking advice and energy from other leaders when considering major organizational decisions or changes. This shows both curiosity and courage. I had the privilege of working closely with Lisa, and we had many conversations about the challenges we were facing. Lisa would always reach out to other leaders to talk through decisions that she faced. She understood that the very best leaders do not have all of the answers, nor do they believe that they do. If a leader believes they have all the answers, it is a sure sign that they are probably a poor leader.

We are all imperfect human beings, and the more we recognize that the better we will be. One of the mistakes that I think many leaders make is that they do not reach out for help, because they see that as a sign of weakness or incompetency. They do not understand that the opposite is true. Reaching out for help comes from a position of strength. That is why it is so important to maintain a network of peer leaders that you can talk to outside of your own organization and have a mentor that you can turn to for advice and guidance. All of the best leaders I have ever known knew when they needed help and sought it out without hesitancy. It shows real commitment to see if somebody else has a better idea or can help you find your way to a better solution than you would on your own.

Gwen McKenzie, former executive with Trinity Health, said that a crucial characteristic of committed leaders when working with others is to "help them find their way, not your way." That says it all. Being a servant leader means helping people find their way. I love it. You are not trying to make everybody a version of you. You are hoping to help them be their best selves. That means they might make different decisions than you would, sometimes those decisions might be better and sometimes they might be worse. But your commitment to helping them be the best leader that they can be will always support the organization being successful. If they get to be themselves, it will unleash their creative energy, their leadership, and their talent and skills, so that great things can happen for them and the people they lead. Organizations that are strictly hierarchical are going away, in my opinion. They do not work, and more and more people are recognizing that. People want to be recognized for their skills, and they want to actively participate in decision-making. They do not want to simply take orders and complete tasks.

I cannot emphasize enough that a leader cannot be loving and compassionate if they are not committed to the eight values discussed in this book. Those you lead will see right through the hypocrisy if you say or do one thing and then not follow through with it in both your professional and personal lives. This can lead to failure for you professionally and personally, as well as for the organization you serve. Why is it so challenging to be committed? Because sometimes commitment is hard. Doing the right thing is hard. Nothing is easy in leadership, but the professional and personal fulfillment is through the roof. I dare say there is no other way to leadership success.

CONCLUSION

ARE YOU NOW EXCITED TO lead with eight compassionate values that will motivate your successful leadership? I hope you agree after reading this book that a leader who emphasizes love and compassion in their daily leadership journey will create a more productive and enjoyable place to work, both for those you lead and for yourself.

This book arrives during a remarkable period of change and upheaval in the way organizations operate. The future of work and the workplace has never been more uncertain, as the shift to remote labor and the virtual office surge to the forefront. It is difficult for a leader who emphasizes working with the people they lead when they cannot be with them in person. Body language and facial expressions are missed on video calls, and it can be more difficult for some people to have honest conversations. We can still be loving and compassionate servant leaders, but sometimes it will be more challenging and will take an extra level of creativity and effort. You must stay fully focused on your team and the matter at hand, though, and model that behavior for your team—and insist on it from them.

Remember that earlier in *Driven by Compassion*, I said that the number one way of breeding distrust in the people you lead is to not listen to them. People often are not listening as intently in virtual meetings, and you cannot be one of them. If anything, you have to be more focused than ever because your interactions with your team members are more limited—and therefore crucial— when they are working remotely. Focus on your leadership values, and you will find that you can translate them to any setting. Remember what I said earlier in the book: the number one sign of distrust is not listening to someone. That includes over a Zoom call.

Below is a sampling of results from a hospital I served as the president and CEO. Over a five-year span, patients that rated the hospital a 10 on a scale of 1 to 10 improved from the 44th percentile to the 64th percentile compared to a benchmark of approximately 1,600 hospitals. Those recommending the hospital improved from the 51st percentile to the 62nd percentile. The hospital also received numerous national quality designations, including being named a Medicare 5 Star Hospital, twice earning Top 50 Heart Hospital honors, and twice earning nursing magnet designation, which only approximately 7 percent of the hospitals in the country achieve for nursing quality. Finally, the organization achieved positive operating margins, which is a strong achievement considering the financial challenges for hospitals to maintain positive operating margins today. Employee turnover remained consistently low, while employee engagement increased slightly.

To be clear, these achievements were the result of the hard work of employees and physicians dedicated to service and excellence, which was the ongoing culture of this organization. However, unless the leadership team did not lead with the eight compassionate values outlined in this book, the metrics would not have improved over the five-plus years I served as the CEO.

It is now time to retake the survey that I asked you to complete in the introductory chapter. Please compare and review your baseline results versus the results from your end-of-book survey. What did your results show? Did the book cause you to change your views on successful people leadership? Did it help you reflect on successful and not so successful leaders you have encountered in your career?

I asked the twenty-five leaders I interviewed for the book to respond to the same survey that you did in the introduction and end of the book. Below are the results of that leader survey to compare with your results.

Please rank the eight compassionate values in order of importance with one being most important and ten the least important. Below are the rankings with the raw mean score:

1. Walk the Talk - 2.91
2. Communication - 3.0
3. Honesty and Integrity - 3.14
4. Servant Leadership - 3.25
5. Trustful - 4.35
6. Commitment - 4.79
7. Patience - 6.15
8. Grudgeless - 6.89

As you can see from this sample, leaders believe that the values of walking the talk, communication, honesty and integrity, and servant leadership are most important. Remember that each of the eight values is absolutely integral to being a successful loving and compassionate leader. These results indicate that being visible, communicating consistently, and living the right values of servant leadership with honesty and integrity are the keys to motivating and supporting those you are entrusted to lead.

Other results of note from the leader survey include the following:

What do you believe is the percentage of CEOs and executives nationally that embrace a loving and compassionate leadership style? The average score was 36 percent. This result clearly shows there is potential for positive growth in this category.

On a scale of 1 to 10 with one being the lowest, do you believe that America's workforce feels valued and heard? The mean score was 4.15. Two critical questions we need to ask ourselves as leaders are: are we listening to our employees? And, if we are, are we valuing what we hear what we hear? This data indicates leaders are failing on this point, and it presents yet another opportunity for loving and compassionate leader skill development.

So, where do you go from here? It starts with a commitment to a leadership style that cares more about people than numbers. No matter what happens in terms of challenges, the numbers will invariably stabilize or improve if those we lead are engaged, motivated, and doing the right thing. I believe that the eight leadership values outlined in this book will support employee engagement and positive operating results.

Joel Manby developed "rules of engagement" for leading with love and compassion. These are keys to utilize during your leadership practice and are as follows:

- ◆ Some will resist and not understand. Love them anyway.
- ◆ Some need to disagree publicly. Be patient anyway.

- Some have been "burned" and are distrustful. Be trusting anyway.
- Some are selfish. Be unselfish anyway.
- Some choose anger. Be forgiving anyway.
- Some may not be dedicated to love and compassion. Be dedicated anyway.
- Set "Do" goals rather than "Be" goals.

Now that you are excited to begin the process of implementing the eight compassionate values that motivate successful leaders, your next step is to write a concise action plan for each value with implementation in thirty days. This would include a review of the plan with your direct supervisor prior to implementation so they can provide support for you. Include in this plan a personalized evaluation matrix to help keep yourself accountable. At the same time, make a genuine attempt to get to personally know all of the employees entrusted to your leadership as a key foundation for your plan.

Some final thoughts: please remember that "a person who feels appreciated will always do more than expected" (anonymous) and "not every productive employee is appreciated but every appreciated employee is productive" (anonymous). Dr. Allen Weiss, former president and CEO of Naples Community Hospital Healthcare System, said that successful "leaders have to love the people they work with." Lisa Reich, vice president and coach at the Studer Group, said that "when all is said and done, all we as leaders have left is the good people we lead."

According to Simon Sinek, an author and speaker, "working hard for something we do not care about is called stress. Working hard for something we love is called passion." President Ronald

Reagan believed that leaders should "live simply, live generously, care deeply, speak kindly, and leave the rest to God."

Your faith in God will provide you the strength and courage to be the ultimate leader who serves with love and compassion for others. This also includes praying for wisdom on a daily basis. According to FaithSearch Partners, wisdom includes "the quality of having experience, good judgment, and knowledge." In the article, "Defining Spiritual Wisdom for Yourself" by everydayhealth.com, it outlines seven tips for achieving spiritual wisdom:

1. Choose wisdom.
2. Trust your instincts.
3. Set boundaries.
4. Surround yourself with wisdom.
5. Learn from your mistakes.
6. Learn from other people's mistakes.
7. Choose it daily.

A belief in wisdom is the rock on which success for the organization, those we lead in a loving and compassionate way, and ourselves is built upon.

Blessings to you for amazing and rewarding success on your personal and professional journey going forward. I am humbly grateful and privileged that you would take the time to read this book and, more importantly, consider this leadership style as part of your everyday work.

ACKNOWLEDGMENTS

Allen Weiss, MD
Ann Stallkamp
Bobbie Shreiner
Carson Dye
Debbie Ritchie
Eugene Meyer
Gary Paxson
Gay Watson Stover
Gene Kaminski
Greg Beykirch
Gwen McKenzie
John V. Bednar
Karen Hartman
Kevin Crowe, MD
Kim Thompson

Leonard (Dave) Frescoln
Lisa Motley
Lisa Reich
Margaret Dimond
Pamela Ream
Patrick Schulte
Philip Weintraub
Phillip A. Incarnati
Richard Cardwell
Richard Flowers
Scott MacLellan
Scott Nygaard, MD
Thomas Stallkamp
William Geschke
Zach Felten